CW00401130

Lily Brett was born in Germa
with her parents in 1948. H
Poems, won the 1987 Vict
poetry, and both her fiction
major prizes, including the 1995 NSW Premier's Award
for fiction for *Just Like That*. Lily Brett is married to the
Australian painter David Rankin. They live in New York.

Lily Brett

New York

PICADOR
Pan Macmillan Australia

First published 2001 in Picador by Pan Macmillan Australia Pty Limited
St Martins Tower, 31 Market Street, Sydney

Reprinted 2001 (twice)

National Library of Australia
cataloguing-in-publication data:

Brett, Lily, 1946– .
New York.

ISBN 0 330 36245 3.

1. New York (N.Y.) – Social life and customs – 20th century.
2. New York (N.Y.) – Anecdotes. I. Title.

974.7104

Typeset in 12/14 pt Bembo by Post Pre-press Group, Brisbane, Queensland
Printed in Australia by McPherson's Printing Group

For David, who shares my New York nights and days.

Contents

New York

New York

No one is frightened of New York anymore. The city, which used to intimidate its own inhabitants, is, today, inhabited by teenagers, mothers, aunties, uncles, shoppers and strollers. No one looks scared.

A decade ago, some New Yorkers wouldn't venture below Fourteenth Street. Now, SoHo has Yves St Laurent and Prada. And people eating ice cream. The bustle of shopping bags and pleasant expressions is so depressing.

Drug dealers and other criminals have been replaced by tourists. Tourists from everywhere. New York seems to be on everyone's itinerary.

I feel almost nostalgic for the old days. For the coke and crack dealers who terrified me. I remember trying to look benign when I passed them on Eleventh Street. I didn't want to be mistaken for a client or a cop.

I miss the people who talked to themselves on the streets, too. There seemed to be someone on each block engrossed in a conversation with an invisible communicant.

I used to pass a middle-aged man in Washington Square Park. His pinstriped suit was immaculately pressed and he carried a leather briefcase. 'You have to let me go, I'm late for work,' he would shout as he strode through the park.

It was always a sobering experience for me. I spent hours wondering what demons were keeping him from where he wanted to go. All of us have something that keeps us from where we dream of being. And it's not a bad thing to be reminded of that.

Today there is little that is disturbing about the city. There is the barrage of greetings that accost you when you enter a store. You have to navigate several greeters to get to the merchandise.

'Hello', 'Welcome', 'How are you doing?', three different people said to me in a shop on West Broadway this morning. The tone in their voices was so friendly, I was perplexed. I thought I must know them.

'Been away travelling?' said another salesperson. I spent two minutes wondering why he thought I'd been away. I'd never been in this store before. The avalanche of warmth and inquiry is disconcerting and tiring.

Shopping in other cities is so much more peaceful. 'In Germany, they leave you alone,' I said to a German friend recently.

She looked black. 'You like this?' she said. 'It drives me crazy when shop assistants ignore me.'

'I find it relaxing, calming,' I said.

The new friendliness in New York also means that stores want you to eat and drink with them. I've been offered iced tea in underwear stores. How do you drink iced tea and try on underwear?

Last week a saleswoman offered me chocolates in a

shoe store. The woman was the width of a sardine. Her hips were slimmer than a cigarette. I declined her offer.

It's hard to feel like a tough New Yorker when all you are trying to avoid is iced tea and chocolate. In the old days, people were impressed if you said you lived in New York. People in Toronto, London and Los Angeles looked at you with awe. You felt tough. A warrior. A survivor.

Now, even the panhandlers have developed a sense of diplomacy. 'You're looking good, Miss,' a man who's been asking for money on my street for years said to me the other day. He took me by surprise.

'Thank you,' I said.

'My pleasure,' he replied.

'New York has lost its edge,' my son who lives in Australia said. Has the city lost its edge? It is still noisy. Still jarring. Still shrill. You can still be knocked down by someone grabbing your taxi. But the city has changed.

'I've got a gun,' a man said to me in a deserted street in Chelsea recently. I looked at him. He was drunk. Very drunk. Too drunk to be dangerous. For a moment, though, I was scared. It was almost a thrill.

Signs

Every day I walk past a sign, on La Guardia Place, that says, *Unnecessary Noise Prohibited*. Every day I wonder how unnecessary must noise be in order to be unnecessary? Only a semantic genius or a Talmudic scholar could interpret this sign, I decide.

For me, most noise is unnecessary. I like silence. The sign seems ineffective, anyway. This stretch of La Guardia Place is no quieter than any other part of the street. Truck and car horns blare just as loudly. Jackhammers still drill and people shout to each other across the street.

Still, the sign cheers me up. It is so stupid. And feeble. It doesn't reflect the city's temperament at all. Unlike the parking signs. *No Parking. No Standing. No Stopping. No Kidding*, says one sign, *Don't even* think *about parking here*, says another. You know you're in New York.

In a city where many of us have too many acquaintances and too few friends, small signs can connect us.

There are signs everywhere in New York. The city is dotted and spotted with signs. There are signs pasted on walls, signs pinned on noticeboards, stuck in store windows, tacked onto trees and posts. There are notices of events, items for sale, pleas for work, offers of jobs.

You can find someone to feed your pet, share your home, read your palm, wash your car, or teach you applied physics or tantric yoga on the average New York noticeboard.

On the surfaces of these odd-sized pieces of paper, you can see into people's lives. And sometimes be perplexed. *Vegetarian non-smoking lesbian would like to share her apartment with a non-smoking heterosexual,* one sign said. Why did this woman want a heterosexual roommate I wondered? Why didn't she want a lesbian? Or a vegetarian? The Wall Street banker who advertised for a clean, early-rising roommate seemed much more straightforward.

Signs can sometimes communicate more intimately than much of our verbal communication. 'I'm lonely,' said a small sign in the corner of the window of an office supplies store. There was a phone number underneath this plaintive announcement. I worried about what sort of people would be responding to that lonely person. And thought it was a worrying sign.

In this largely impersonal city, there are intimacies and personal revelations in unlikely and unexpected places. A sign pinned on a pear tree on Eighth Street read, *Missing: White silky terrier. Reward $500. Owner very distressed.*

I knew things were going downhill when two days later, the sign was changed. *Missing: White silky terrier. Reward $500. Owner heartbroken.*

I've seen apartments for rent advertised on trees. If you're looking for a place to live, copying a phone number from a tree trunk can prove more effective than seeing a real-estate broker. Apartments, which are scarce and expensive, change hands in strangely personal ways.

Sometimes the signs are not small at all. A large sign near one of the city's tunnels says *Trucks With Overweight Permit*. I used to gaze at this sign and think that it might be useful if they could distribute overweight permits to people, too. Quite a few of us could be cheered up with permission of this sort.

A sign in a local cafe haunted me for a long time. *Missing*, the sign said, *Three-legged black and white mongrel. Blind in one eye, damaged tail, missing one ear. Castrated last week. Answers to 'Lucky'*. A photograph of Lucky, looking not too beleaguered, accompanied the notice.

For weeks, I kept a lookout for Lucky. I looked for him on my early morning walks along the Hudson. I looked for him when I went to the drycleaners, or to the corner store. I looked for him in Chinatown and Little Italy.

The sign about him being missing stayed up for months. I don't know if he was ever found.

Chinatown

I love Chinatown. Chinatown is like a touchstone, a link with reality, which is necessary when you live in a city like New York.

A city in which people don't blink at spending two thousand dollars on a dress for their teenage daughter. And scores of pubescent girls shop at Prada, Todd Oldham and Dolce & Gabbana. A city in which it is not uncommon for restaurant bills to add up to hundreds or more dollars. Inhabitants of a city like this need a reality check.

It's too easy to feel swamped by the city. By the frantic pace, by the furious networking, day and night. By the feeling that your value and your importance is calculated in terms of what you have achieved and who you know.

Do you know the right people? If you don't, you don't matter. You can be discarded, snubbed and overlooked. In New York it is not hard to feel that everyone shares these values. In New York it is easy to think that your existence is also what other people are experiencing.

Chinatown cures you of this. It is full of life. Ordinary life. It has everything that ordinary life is composed of. And it always calms me.

I'm soothed by the grandmothers with their grand-children. By the elderly couples. By the teenagers and young children, who all seem to speak Chinese.

I'm soothed by the markets and shops and food stalls and restaurants. By all the eating and talking.

I shop in Chinatown. I buy my fruit and vegetables there. The prices are always a quarter of what they are in SoHo, which borders on Chinatown.

I sometimes buy fish, although I'm put off by the fact that most of the fish are still moving. And some of them are trying to jump out of buckets. I once saw a large crab making a dash for freedom on the corner of Grand Street and The Bowery.

I like Chinatown at night, too. It is always busy. Full of people. Workers pour out of factories and sweatshops.

Watching them reminds me of what a privileged life I lead. I know something about factories and sweatshops. Both of my parents worked in factories. We were refugees to Australia. My parents worked long hours behind sewing machines, and, of course, were exploited. The sewing machines and the low pay put an end to my mother's dream of becoming a paediatrician.

I watch the Chinese workers buy their food. I know they still have to go home and cook it. Others stop at a hot-food vendor and eat on the spot.

In Chinatown, people are always eating. They eat in restaurants, in cafes and in the streets. Food is cooked and served at a furious pace.

On the street, people fry and steam and toss and chop in impossibly small spaces. They produce miraculous food in these makeshift kitchens. It is so delicious. And so cheap.

One of my favourite places in Chinatown is Maria's Bakery on Lafayette Street. Don't be deceived by the name. There is nothing Italian about Maria's. It is wholly Chinese. Maria's is not chic. It is not upmarket. It is a working-class cafe and restaurant. The customers are almost all Chinese. There are not many European faces at Maria's.

Apart from the meals, which are good and absurdly cheap, you can buy brightly coloured ice-cream cakes and an assortment of oddly Anglo-Saxon white-bread sandwiches.

I can sit at Maria's for hours and watch families eating. Mothers, fathers, grandparents and children. All eating and talking. The different generations seem so at ease with each other.

It gives me a peacefulness, a sense of wellbeing, to be in the middle of this familial harmony. I feel good when I leave. And if I've managed to avoid eating more than one black-bean bun, I feel even better.

The Country

I woke up with an urge to get out of the city. To see some countryside. To see more sky. This urge was unusual for me. I'm quite urban. Loneliness often overtakes me if I'm out of the city.

Still, I felt restless, hemmed in. 'Let's go away for the weekend,' I said to my husband. We decided on Bethlehem, Pennsylvania. I liked the notion of travelling to Bethlehem. This Bethlehem is two hours from New York.

We hired a car. A Ford Explorer. Like most New Yorkers, we rarely drive. Hiring a car feels exciting. I get into the Ford Explorer. I feel happy. So far, the weekend is working out well.

Ten minutes after we've left Manhattan, I feel hungry. Travelling makes me hungry. I've packed some food. I open the food bag. My husband looks over and raises his eyebrows. I've packed bottled water, bananas, carrots, apples, bread and cheese. 'We're not going to Mars,' he says. He notices popcorn stuffed into a side pocket.

'Why did you bring popcorn?' he asks. 'You can get popcorn everywhere they sell anything.'

'Not this particular brand,' I say.

We drive in silence for a while. I eat an apple and some carrots. The landscape already looks rural. Not many houses. Lots of trees. I miss New York. I always miss New York when I leave. I often miss New York before I've left. I miss the city when I'm still packing. I forget about the stench in some parts of the city when the weather warms up. I forget about the crowds and the tension.

We're passing more trees. 'Pennsylvania has a lot of trees,' I say to my husband.

'I've seen pear trees, pine trees, magnolias, firs and dogwoods,' he says.

'Are all these trees necessary?' I say to him.

We're surrounded by green. So much green. Green everywhere. I don't like green. I feel carsick. Greensick. I don't like trees that much. Last year, we visited friends in San Francisco. They took us to the Redwood National Park. The redwood trees were ancient and tall. Very tall. I felt anxious and oppressed. I couldn't look up without feeling bilious. I revived when we left the forest and found a cafe.

I'm not at ease in the country. And the country isn't at ease with me. Everything that can fly bites me. Every gnat, wasp, mosquito, fly or flea that can bite bites me. If butterflies and moths could bite they would bite me, too.

And I respond to the bites. I swell up. I come out in welts and bumps. They're hot and they itch for days. I can't sleep. I lie in bed itching. I've tried ice packs on the bites and given myself frostbite.

Last summer, on Shelter Island, a small island two hours east of New York, I wore an insect repellent bracelet. The bracelet was supposed to ward off all insects in the vicinity for thirty hours. I was bitten after two minutes.

I put on more bracelets. One around each wrist, two on each ankle and one in my hair. The bracelets looked like hospital identification tags. I looked like an escapee from a lunatic asylum. I wore the tags all summer.

In Bethlehem, we check in to a charming inn. We take a walk. Bethlehem is very pretty. It has a river and quaint old buildings. I enjoy the walk. But I'm not comfortable. We go to bed early.

In the morning, I feel isolated and dislocated. I ask the innkeeper if the local ambulance carries a defibrillator. 'Do you have heart disease?' he asks.

'No,' I say. 'Just inquiring.'

We leave Bethlehem earlier than we intended. Approaching New York, we pass four police cars, their blue lights flashing, in a huddle at the side of the road. I feel much better.

Discarding

Some people look forward to new things. I don't. It doesn't matter what it is. A new year, a new coat, a new house. I feel sad about giving up the old. I mourn the old year, the old coat, the old house.

I feel worried about the new. I don't like change. I don't like surprises. And I don't like the unknown. I know the unknown is part of the human experience. Part of the human condition. But I don't like it.

I like to know. The more I know about a friend, the more comfortable I feel. I sometimes think I make friends uncomfortable by how much I want to know about them.

In New York, it's easy to know nothing much about someone you've known for years.

I like to know people's rituals and routines. I like to know what they have for lunch. I like familiarity. I find it reassuring.

I like the fact that Joe's Dairy, in Sullivan Street, always closes for lunch. Joe's Dairy, a cheese shop, has been in SoHo for years. They make hundreds of pounds of fresh and smoked mozzarella there every day. And every day they close between 12 p.m. and 1 p.m. for lunch.

Joe's Dairy is one of the last remnants of the old neighbourhood left. There are not that many of the old neighbours themselves left. SoHo used to be full of artists and writers. Now it seems the only artists or writers who are left are married to bankers or lawyers.

Last New Year's Eve, SoHo looked like it used to look. The streets were almost deserted except for a few locals. It was so quiet and peaceful. I felt so happy despite the fact that the whole new year, new century, new millennium, was one new thing too many for me.

I was used to the old millennium, the old century. I was daunted by so many new beginnings. To embrace the new, what was it necessary to discard? The old? The past? The question bothered me.

I have trouble discarding things. I'm not overly attached to objects. I don't hoard things. I don't get upset if a glass or plate or vase breaks. I don't care about those things.

My parents understood the limited value of material possessions. In Auschwitz, the only thing that each of them owned was their soul. It was the only thing they were left with. And the most crucial.

It was hard to place too much importance on accumulating objects in our house. The tables and chairs or desks or toys were not what was important. I have, on the whole, retained that attitude. I don't become attached to these things.

It's the more personal possessions I have trouble parting with. I have two pairs of my late mother's shoes in my closet. I guard them as though my mother's feet were still in them.

I have kept flowers I have been given until they're not only dead, they're disintegrating. I've looked at bunches of dead roses and seen them as forlorn ballerinas, dilapidated bridesmaids. And had to ask someone else to throw them out.

The voice mail on my cellular phone is almost clogged because I can't discard certain messages. Messages from my husband and children. I can't delete them. I keep saving them. It's a bit pathetic. Soon no one will be able to leave me a new message. I have to learn to discard them.

Sometimes it is us who are discarded. I hate that. I hate it when someone suddenly decides they don't like me. When someone I've been friendly with is suddenly unfriendly. With no warning and no explanation. It unnerves me.

I think parents often feel unnerved and discarded. There's a certain age up to which children need you, and after that they start discarding you. That can be hard to get used to.

I wept when my youngest daughter moved to Philadelphia to go to college. I didn't know I was going to be overjoyed to be childless. Some new experiences are entirely exhilarating.

The Car

This summer, my car broke down in the supermarket car park on the first day I'd been to Shelter Island in months.

Shelter Island is a quiet place. I spend some of each summer there. The pace of the island is reflected in the contents of the Police Blotter, a page which appears weekly in the *Shelter Island Reporter*.

This week, the Police Blotter reported three separate incidents in which a deer was hit by a vehicle. There was also news of a complaint that had been received about a barking dog, and the news that a telephone worker had been attacked by a turkey. 'The owner of the assailant restrained the bird. No charges were filed,' the newspaper stated.

I felt so irritated when the car we keep on the island broke down. I had been looking forward to some peace and solitude. I kept turning the key in the ignition in an effort to restart the car. There was no sound from the engine. It was a futile mission.

I only like my car when it works. Any feelings of warmth I'd once had for this car had been rapidly cooling since the car started falling apart.

It is a 1986 Lincoln Continental. It is supposed to do many things. It is supposed to tell you the outside temperature and the direction you are travelling in. But the temperature that comes up on the car's electronic system never matches the weather. And the car's sense of direction is definitely skewed. No matter which way you turn, the car tells you you are travelling north or northwest. I've turned full circles, and made myself dizzy, in order to see if the car can detect that we are now facing south or south-east. It never has.

When the car broke down in the supermarket car park, I was furious. It was the last straw. I glared at the car. Nothing happened. It's as hard to intimidate a car as it is to intimidate your adult children. I got out of the car and kicked one of the tyres. I didn't feel better.

I tried to calm down. To remember that I come here to feel calmer. To do ordinary things. Like call and wait for a car mechanic.

'Car not working?' a man walking by asked me. I nodded glumly.

'I think it's the car battery,' I said. He left to get some jumper leads from his car.

By the time he got back, five minutes later, three people had offered to go and get a car mechanic. But the jumper leads did the trick. The car started. I backed out of my parking spot. I had just enough time to feel triumphant before the car came to a stop. I was still in the car park. I got out.

The general consensus in the car park was that I

needed a new battery. The atmosphere around my broken-down vehicle was quite festive. I realised I was enjoying myself. Everyone was so cheerful and so friendly. There was a better atmosphere in the supermarket car park than there is at most dinner parties. An hour after my car first broke down, I'd made quite a few new friends.

Eventually the car started. I drove off to the car mechanic's. The car broke down three more times before I got there. Each time people pulled up to ask what was wrong. Everyone was concerned. Men and women checked out the car's engine.

By the time I'd had a new battery installed, it was late afternoon. I hadn't been to the beach where I usually sit and stay alert for sand flies and gnats because I react badly to bites. I hadn't swum in the pond and tried not to think about the snapping turtle who lives there. I'd had the best day in the country I'd had in years.

Germs

Instead of withdrawing money, the man ahead of me at the automated teller machine was cleaning the equipment. He was scrubbing the screen with several wet towelettes.

He wasn't a cleaner. He looked more like a lawyer or an accountant. I was in a hurry. I cleared my throat, impatiently, several times. He took no notice.

He finished the screen and began to wipe down the keypad. He unwrapped some more towelettes. I looked at the packet. They were disposable, anti-bacterial towelettes.

I wasn't unsympathetic to this man's needs. I've been known to press elevator buttons with my elbows if someone unsavoury has pressed them before me. I've developed unusually dexterous elbows.

I'm not obsessive about using my elbows. I usually don't do it if anyone else is present. In company, I like to appear relaxed and casual.

I have a friend who is decidedly unrelaxed about what can happen if you touch the wrong button. Last winter, at the height of the flu season, she arrived at my door with a gift. A bottle of instant hand sanitiser.

I tried to look pleased. 'Everything you touch, outside the house, has been touched by hundreds of others,' she said. 'Every escalator rail, supermarket trolley or door handle has been handled by someone else. There are germs everywhere.'

The instant hand sanitiser promised to kill 99.99 per cent of most common germs, germs that cause illness, in less than fifteen seconds. 'Maybe we should swallow it as well,' I said. 'That way we could avoid all illness.' She looked offended. I put the hand sanitiser straight into my handbag to appease her.

A few weeks later, I was at the Cort Theatre. To see David Hare's play, *The Blue Room*, starring Nicole Kidman. Tickets had been hard to get. The show was almost sold out before it opened.

This situation was causally connected to the fact that Miss Kidman spent most of her time on stage partially disrobed. And, for a brief moment, was completely naked.

Inside the theatre, I noticed that many of the patrons were carrying binoculars and opera glasses.

On stage, Miss Kidman was a sight to behold. With and without her clothes. She was tall, slim, blonde and blemishless. How could any body have so few blemishes and bumps? She was perfectly taut and perfectly smooth. There was not even a minuscule ripple of cellulite in sight.

I leaned over and asked the woman sitting in front of me if I could borrow her binoculars. The woman looked unnerved. As if I'd asked to borrow her underpants or her lipstick. 'I won't lick them,' I said in what I hoped was a humorous tone. She handed me the binoculars, reluctantly.

Close up Nicole Kidman looked even better. It was a bit depressing. I returned the binoculars almost immediately. The woman took her binoculars back, and started cleaning them. She was using wet towelettes, from a silver sachet. Like the man at the cash machine.

I watched in the dark as she cleaned every square millimetre of the binoculars and then cleaned her hands. I missed ten minutes of the play watching her cleaning.

I was drawn back to the action on stage when Miss Kidman's co-star, Iain Glen, suddenly catapulted himself into a cartwheel. He, too, was in the nude. A nude man mid-cartwheel is a not uninteresting vision.

The cartwheel and Miss Kidman's body were the best parts of the play. It was a loveless, detached piece of theatre. And I'm tired of seeing men's fantasies about what women want, and what men want to do to them.

'Thank you for lending me your binoculars,' I said to the woman in front of me at the end of the evening.

'You can get colds and flus and hepatitis and tuberculosis from touching other people's things,' she said to me, quite sternly.

'Really?' I replied.

I started to feel anxious. And tense. I reached into my handbag. The hand sanitiser was still in there. Maybe I should use it now and then, I thought. That thought eased my tension.

Messages

It's not cyberspace, the Internet, the web, or any inter-galactic or interplanetary method of transporting messages that disturbs my wellbeing.

The questions that are raised about modern communications systems, and their effects on us, are not questions that bother me.

I can't get overly excited about planets and transmitting stations. Those forms of communication are not what I'm most familiar with. But I am not disturbed by their instant, and far-reaching, dispatches and communiqués.

I am much more bothered by the more ordinary ways we say things to each other. I am much more perturbed by the more subtle modes of interaction we employ and utilise.

New York is the epicentre of coded words and loaded conversation and finely calibrated and calculated methods of communication. Everything rests on your status and your importance. Every New Yorker is more important than someone they deal with and every New Yorker can evaluate a person's value, within seconds.

In a phone call, you can be put on hold, or connected to the voice mail of the person you've called, or told you'll be called back, or put straight through.

Not being able to get your calls returned shows you exactly where you stand. And it is meant to. It is a loud and clear statement of your lack of importance. You have to be able to tolerate this humiliation. At least until your ratings rise.

Last week I rang someone who had agreed to do me a favour. He is a well-connected public relations man. I rang him five or six times. Each time his secretary said he would call me back. He never did. By the end of the ordeal, I hated him. And definitely felt my own insignificance.

I spent two days trying to work out how I could make the public relations man feel bad, before I gave up and realised it was a lost cause.

The most effective ways of affecting people come from aspects of ourselves that are much more powerful than any high-tech gadgetry. Although sometimes the language that comes out of my computer can be very affecting.

The following addresses had permanent fatal errors, my computer told me recently. It was referring to email I'd sent. I didn't like the words permanent and fatal placed next to each other. It unnerved me for the rest of the day.

Another time the computer announced, *Host not found.* The thought of a lost host upset me. I wish the computer used less harsh language.

I changed email servers because my computer kept telling me I was idle whenever I paused to think. I'm fairly hard working. I couldn't stand the accusations of idleness.

I'm clearly moved by what appears on my screen. Technology doesn't leave me cold. Although I was slow to appreciate the benefits of fibre-optic connections. I had to be nagged for years to get email. Now I love it.

In the beginning I signed myself Lilycyberchick and felt very hip. If you say it fast, it sounds Russian or Polish.

But nothing in cyberspace measures up to what we can do to each other on the ground. Few things can be as powerful as a snub or a glare or a loving expression. These small actions are more potent than any exchange in space.

Gifts can also be a powerful form of communication. Gifts can be very articulate utterances. A gift can convey so much more than what appears on the surface. Presents can be vehicles to deliver hostile messages. Like giving someone who's drowning in domesticity a new set of tea towels. Or buying a person a garment two sizes too large. Or too small.

A friend who'd gained a lot of weight in her pregnancy, was given the tiniest pair of lace underpants by her very svelte mother. What was her mother thinking?

One of my daughters gave me a brooch that said *Halfhearted* when our relationship was going through a rough patch. I knew exactly how this daughter felt about me.

Cher's Mother

I've been looking at myself in the mirror more frequently recently.

As a rule, I don't like mirrors. My husband says I pull a face each time I look at myself in the mirror. He says I grimace at my reflection. He tells me I can't possibly know what I look like as I always see my features distorted and twisted.

I think a lot of women do this. Frown or pout or scowl at themselves. As though what we're seeing doesn't quite match our expectations.

For a while, I tried looking neutral whenever I approached a mirror, but it didn't work. My face looked stiff as though rigor mortis was about to set in. So I began avoiding mirrors as much as I could. Until recently.

What precipitated the change was an experience in Düsseldorf. I was in Düsseldorf as part of a small book tour of Germany and Austria. I decided to go to the hairdresser's. To have the expensive, natural-looking, art-fully applied highlights and tones in my hair colour replenished.

A friend had recommended the salon. The young man who was assigned to do my hair looked competent. He began applying the coiour. I began to read a book I had brought. Five minutes later, I caught him looking at me quizzically. 'You look like Cher's mother,' he said to me, quite excitedly. I was startled. I thought I must have mis-heard him. What had he said? I look like Cher's mother?

'You look like Cher's mother,' he repeated and beamed. I looked at him. Maybe it was his English? Maybe he meant to say Cher's sister? 'Many people must say you look like Cher's mother,' he said to me.

My heart sank. He did mean Cher's mother. I looked at myself in the mirror. I did look a bit pale. But Cher's mother? Surely I couldn't look like Cher's mother? My spirits started to slump. Cher and I are exactly the same age. I looked at myself again. I looked even paler, and older.

'Hasn't anyone told you you look like Cher's mother?' the young man said, perplexed.

'No,' I said curtly and buried my head in my book.

He wasn't deterred. 'Don't you think she looks like Cher's mother?' he asked loudly, looking around at several people in the salon. I was in luck. No one appeared to speak English. There was no reply.

The resemblance to Cher has been remarked on before. But it was always a resemblance to Cher herself.

I have a small history with Cher. I interviewed her decades ago. I was a young rock journalist. She borrowed my diamanté-lined false eyelashes. She looked fabulous in them.

I tried to read my book, but I felt depressed. And I felt stupid for feeling depressed. I knew there were more important things in life than whether you looked like Cher or Cher's mother.

But the thought dogged me all day. I thought about it in the middle of a radio interview I was doing. I thought about it in taxis. I thought about it while I was trying to get some exercise power walking along the Rhine.

I felt annoyed with myself for not being able to get the thought out of my head. I wanted to go back to the salon and hit the young man. Why did he have to say I looked like Cher's mother?

By the end of the day, I was demoralised and exhausted. I went back to my hotel. It was one of those hotels with the sort of grey, grim fluorescent lighting in the rooms that strips your spirit, and mirrors in the elevators that make you look like Dracula before he's been topped up with blood.

I asked my publisher if I could change hotels. She said I was in this hotel because there were several big conventions in town and no hotel rooms available.

By the time I went to bed I felt like Cher's grandmother.

Matchmaking

Relationships are so difficult today. So many factors now play a part in partnerships. There are so many more things to consider than the question of being in love.

Jobs and their location come into the equation. You can't marry a man who lives in Texas if you work in New York. Potential living arrangements pose more problems. In many cities a good apartment can be harder to find than a good partner. And more prized. You have to be madly in love to give up an apartment for a partner.

Even sex has become more confusing, with a broader range of sexual persuasion and gender. So many more permutations and combinations are possible, and acceptable.

The days when sex was merely forbidden seem simple. Innocent.

Sex is so complicated now. The act itself, and making

time for it. A recent *New Yorker* cartoon shows a late middle-aged couple in their living room. 'Now that the kids are grown and gone, I thought it might be a good time for us to have sex,' the man is saying. That cartoon made many of us laugh.

There are also children to contend with. Before any commitment. Many people have to court and date as parents. The existence of a child has to be taken into account in the plans and calculations of possible relationships.

A friend of mine was invited, by her lover, to Ibiza for the summer. 'Where will I sleep?' she said to me. 'I have a son. He has a daughter. We can't just present ourselves as a couple to the children.

'I'll sleep in his guest room,' she said, answering her own question. 'I don't have to have wild sex every night,' she added.

I was impressed by the fact that wild sex was on her mind, if not on her daily agenda. I was pleased, too. My friend was single for quite a while. New York is full of single people. Of the seven-and-a-half million people in New York City, just over three million are single.

Forty-eight per cent of the city's households consist of single people. This is the highest concentration in the United States. With the exception of a leper colony in Hawaii.

I've played my part in attempting to change these statistics. I've been an inveterate matchmaker all my life. I'm not sure why.

I have tried to matchmake my widowed father. I've tried to find him a wife. He doesn't want one. But I haven't let that deter me. I know he is lonely. And he loves doing things for others. He's got a great sense of humour. And he's a very good dancer. His loneliness would go if he had a partner.

I tried to matchmake him with a woman I'd never met. That was a mistake. He just didn't like her. My father only went on the date to please me. Why can't I please him and allow him to be single?

I've tried to matchmake so many people. In another life I must have been a marriage broker. A very mediocre broker. I have a dismal record of pairing people. I've introduced people who disliked each other so much that neither spoke to me again.

My biggest success has been one marriage. There is a small coda to this success story. They divorced after four years.

I should leave the matchmaking business to those who know what they're doing.

Matchmaking services are flourishing here. And women are flocking to them.

Having once been attached to a man adds some weight in society's rankings for women. A divorced woman carries more cache in the social stakes than one who has never been married. A man, on the other hand, who has remained single, will be viewed as attractive and eligible until the day he is buried. It is so annoying.

The situation becomes advantageous, however, if you have an unattached man available. And I have. My father.

Memory

Memory is such a strange thing. It activates, recalls, recolours, enlarges and reduces events and occasions. It brings back facts and fictions, mistakes and misgivings. It stores dreams and hopes and embarrassments and indignities.

It is like a large closet. A repository for used and yet-to-be-used thoughts and knowledge. It is an accumulation of all that we are and some of what we hope to be.

You can retrieve whatever you choose to. Or can you?

Why are some things so easy to remember? So easy to recollect? And why are others so hard to summon up? Why do some memories linger for longer than you want them to?

Humiliations and sadnesses, it seems to me, are never hard to retrieve. And always difficult to get rid of.

Why can't you revive the memory of something funny as easily? Why are we so readily reminded of things that bother us? Most of us can recall our teenage loneliness and ignominy in a second. We can remember the snubs, the rebuffs and the mortification. Why? What purpose does this serve? And why is fear so easy to remember? And happiness so hard to retrace? I wish I knew.

I know memory changes with understanding. Understanding imbues memory with new shades and meanings. I've seen this clearly. My mother's vanity was so much easier to comprehend when I grew up and understood that a terrible past had taken almost everything but her beauty from her. This understanding altered many of my memories about my mother.

Memories are often selective. We bring up what suits us. It must suit me to be morose. I can recall any distressing event in two seconds. I don't have to dredge it up. It's there, lying in wait for my summons.

I wish I didn't need these distressing remembrances and reminders. I wish I wasn't attached to these mementos and souvenirs and keepsakes of ordeals and tribulations. I wish I could discard all prompters and flashbacks of past misery and melancholia. But the matter of what we discard and what we save is so complicated.

I could undergo another hundred years of analysis and still not have enough clarity about my penchant for sadness and difficulty.

My memories clearly reflect my disposition and my vision. For me fear and apprehension are much easier to locate than joy and anticipation. I wish I could change this.

I have instant access to sadness. If I overhear two bars of Pavarotti singing an aria from *Tosca* or *La Traviata*, I start crying. The arias remind me of my mother. She died fourteen years ago. When I hear Pavarotti, I see my mother, humming the arias to herself in the kitchen as she washes dishes.

The area in the East Village where we lived for our first year in New York is resonant with memory for me. We knew no one when we moved here. And I was so nervous of this city. I'd read stories of shootings and muggings and heartless New Yorkers.

We ate in a forlorn fluorescent-lit deli every night for the first two weeks. We had a tiny kitchen and no kitchen equipment.

I was too nervous to venture further than my immediate neighbourhood. Which was a mistake. Almost any other neighbouring area would have been more uplifting than the one we lived in. There were drug dealers and drug addicts on every corner. And people talking to themselves.

The East Village is not the same place now. It has changed completely. It is full of young people and cafes and parks and gardens. I often go there. I like the ambience.

I was there last week. I was waiting for the lights to change on Second Avenue, when all of a sudden the sound of Roy Orbison singing 'Only The Lonely' filled the street corner. The music was coming from a retro clothing store. I found myself mouthing the lyrics. I was transported. I was fifteen again. I walked all the way down Second Avenue smiling.

Lines

'Walking fast will line your face,' a neighbour said to me. She had stopped me on West Broadway to tell me this.

'Really?' I said.

'I'm a firm believer in that,' she answered.

I looked at her face. She is sixtysomething. Her face was relatively unlined. 'I've seen you,' she said. 'You walk everywhere at high speed.'

She is right. I do. I love walking fast. Walking fast is not all that easy a feat to accomplish in the increasingly crowded streets of Manhattan.

'I love walking fast,' I said to my neighbour. She looked disapproving. This neighbour once asked me to join her at her regular meditation sessions. I declined. I explained that meditation made me nervous. Made me anxious. She wasn't that friendly after that.

'I never walk fast,' she said to me. 'It causes frowning. And frowning creates lines and wrinkles.'

I spotted a loophole in her theory. 'But I love it,' I said to her. 'I'm sure I look happy when I'm walking. I'm sure I'm not frowning.' I said this with conviction. But after I'd left her, some doubts set in. I felt worried. This worry about possible frowning and wrinkling put a dent in my enthusiasm for walking for days.

I strained to catch glimpses of myself in reflections while I was walking. I tried to check my facial expression in store windows and car windscreens. Each time I managed to see myself, I was frowning.

'You can always have plastic surgery,' Geoffrey, the man who cuts my hair, said to me. I'd asked him if he'd noticed a disproportionate increase in the lines on my face in the last two or three years.

I ignored his comment. I can't be rude to him. This man is crucial to me. My hair is curly. It's not easy to get curls to aim themselves in whimsical directions and attractive angles. To make curls look carefree requires a skilful hairdresser.

Geoffrey is an expert on plastic surgery. He cuts hair on the Upper East Side. He knows the name of the best plastic surgeon for every known body part. He talks about liposuction for thighs and chins, and eyelid readjustment and stomach reconstruction, as though he was talking about the weather.

'You look good,' I said to him to put an end to the plastic surgery conversation. And he did. He's a good-looking young man. He's always dressed in Gucci and Prada. He wears designer label clothes and watches. I've admired his growing collection of Cartier and Rolex for years.

Hairdressing is not what it used to be. This thirty-four-year-old man earns more money than most doctors.

'You look good,' I repeated. I could see Geoffrey was still thinking of plastic surgery possibilities he felt could benefit me.

'Yeah, I do look good,' he said. 'I've just had another round of botulism injections.'

'You've had botulism injections?' I said. I had read in the *New York Times* that botulism injections were becoming popular. The botulism is injected into various parts of the face. It paralyses the muscles. Stops people from frowning or squinting or grimacing. It gives skin a smoother appearance.

Botulism had a bad name when it was only seen as a severe, and sometimes fatal, form of food poisoning. Now botulism is being embraced. By many people. Businessmen are lining up for botulism injections. They feel the injections give them an edge during difficult negotiations. All their tension is masked by an immobile expression.

The effect of the botulism wears off after six months. After six months, you need a new series of injections. Geoffrey had had his forehead and the area around his eyes injected. 'It doesn't hurt that much,' he said. 'Although it feels weird for the first couple of days. You want to frown but you can't.'

I walked home from the salon. It's a long walk. Over eighty blocks. I walked fast, and contemplated botulism injections.

Family

My eighty-four-year-old father is considering having an operation on his prostate. A not uncommon operation for men his age. He has called me to discuss the advantages and disadvantages.

I am worried. I don't want him to be operated on unnecessarily. 'It's not a big deal,' he says. 'Except,' he adds after a few seconds, 'I could be impotent after the operation.'

I feel uneasy. I'd feel more comfortable discussing the dangers of anaesthesia than the potential impotence of a parent. 'Oh,' I say for lack of a better response. I try to make it a sympathetic 'Oh'.

'It doesn't matter,' my father says, a bit forlornly. 'I don't have anyone to have sex with anyway.' I take a deep breath. This is not a conversation I care to continue.

'So, I might be impotent. So what?' my father says with a sudden flourish. I can see that he is trying to make the best of the situation. 'It's not important,' he says, not quite convincingly.

I tell a friend about my father's problem. 'He could be impotent if he has the operation,' I say.

'Well he's certainly had his fair share of sex,' she says. I am surprised. She doesn't know my father. I realise she is confusing my father with the father in my novels. I don't correct her. I don't want to remove the sexual frisson from my father's image. I briefly wonder what constitutes a fair share of sex.

My son calls to discuss my father's condition. I tell him I've decided to try and dissuade my father from going ahead with the operation. My son tells me other news. His friend, Roger V., has been depressed and is on Prozac. 'He feels much better now,' my son says. 'But he can't have orgasms.'

'Oh,' I say.

'It's a common side effect,' my son says. 'A big price to pay for feeling better. Orgasms are one of life's true pleasures.'

I feel myself reddening. How did the conversation career into this area? I realise I haven't replied. 'Of course,' I say hastily.

Later in the day, I am walking on Fifth Avenue with my younger daughter. It is early evening. This part of Fifth Avenue is filled with New York University students. I like being in student areas. The air seems more intellectual, more vibrant, more hopeful.

'Most guys I know don't want oral sex,' a young woman we are passing says to her friend. I am stunned. I turn around to take another look at the girl who is airing this information. She is young. About nineteen. The guy she is talking to doesn't look bothered. He just nods.

As though they are talking about train timetables.

I've stopped walking. And am just staring. My daughter looks in the girl's direction. 'Who has she been going out with?' my daughter says in a voice laced with sarcasm. I look at my daughter. What is she saying?

'All guys want oral sex,' my daughter says. I'm speechless. She's twenty-four. She's the baby of the family. What does she know about this? What has she been doing? I feel shaky. I start walking. 'All guys want oral sex,' she says again, and laughs. I walk faster. My daughter runs to catch up with me. 'It's okay to talk about this,' she says.

I try to calm down. Since the impeachment trial, oral sex has been discussed in classrooms, churches and on television. The subject shouldn't make me nervous. 'At least the impeachment trial has improved the quality of New York street conversation,' I say to my daughter. And it's true. For years street conversations were not a patch on what they used to be. They were mostly about shopping. Before that you could overhear fascinating snippets. Riveting morsels and slivers of other people's lives.

You could hear men and women talking about their landlords, their mothers, their lovers, their bank accounts, their therapists and analysts. Therapists and analysts. Tame topics, though, next to impotency, orgasm and oral sex.

Non-fat

I tried to buy some non-fat yogurt on the first day of my first book tour in Germany. It was about two years ago. Book tours can require a lot of eating. A lot of lunch and dinner engagements. I have to be careful. I merely have to look at food and my hips thicken.

I'd shipped over some fat-free cereal before the tour began. I'd warned everyone at my publisher's that they were not to laugh when the cereal arrived. They fell about laughing. I didn't think it was that funny.

I looked for the non-fat yogurt. I looked and looked. It wasn't easy to find. I decided an expensive food store was the answer. I was in Munich at the time. I chose a food store that reeked of expense. A gourmet store.

Everything was artfully arranged. Artichokes lay in beautiful baskets. The radishes resembled rubies. The grapes were clustered and tied in bunches like brides-maids' bouquets. The display of apples and pears looked like a Renoir painting. This was not a store. This was more like a food museum. I knew I was in the right place. This store would have everything.

I asked for non-fat yogurt. The woman behind the counter looked perplexed. 'Without fat,' I said in my best German. The woman nodded. She went off and returned with a tub of yogurt. I felt happy. Pleased with myself. Until I noticed *3.8% Fat* written on top of the yogurt container. 'Without fat,' I said, again, to the woman who had served me.

She shook her head. 'With fat is much better,' she said. The store didn't stock non-fat yogurt another assistant told me.

This experience was repeated in several cities. Hamburg, Frankfurt, Düsseldorf, Leipzig. I remembered that an American had told me that non-fat yogurt was hard to get in France and in Italy.

I looked for low-fat yogurt. It was still hard to find, but it was available. The lowest fat content I found was 0.3 per cent, in a supermarket in Berlin.

Germans all around me were eating their 3.8 per cent yogurt. And butter. I watched in admiration and envy as a German businessman piled cheese on top of his heavily buttered bread. He wasn't fat. And neither were most Germans. Not next to Americans. Why not?

Americans are getting bigger. Bigger and wider. Americans, the *Washington Post* said, used to require eighteen inches of space to sit comfortably in. Now they need more. And more. A Seattle theatre installed some twenty-four-inch seats and trained their ushers to subtly steer larger patrons to the larger seats.

A car seat manufacturer here has reduced the size of its car cushions. This has left more room for hips and thighs. And some airlines have installed higher tray tables above their seats. Tables that won't pinch a protruding stomach.

America is the home of the free and the brave, the national anthem says. It is also the home of fat-free. You can get fat-free everything in America. You can get fat-free sausage and fat-free baked ham. You can get fat-free cookies and fat-free cheesecake. You can get fat-free dog and cat food. You can probably get fat-free fish food, too.

I'd packed my fat-free cereal in plastic bags, in breakfast-sized portions. 'You are American,' a waitress in Frankfurt said as she watched me struggling with the cereal. I tried to look dignified. It's hard when you're pouring cereal into a bowl from a plastic bag.

I ditched the low-fat yogurt and fat-free cereal for the last few days of the tour. I enjoyed every gram of fat in each of my breakfasts. I didn't care if I gained weight.

Half of all Americans are overweight and a third are obese. With all of the reduced-fat and less-fat and low-fat and non-fat food available, how can that be? Why aren't the French and Italians and Germans, who live in a calorie-filled universe, bigger than Americans? It's a puzzle to me.

Women

Women are not generous to each other. I hate to say it. It seems a shocking statement. Something that is not often voiced. But it is true. And I am sure it is not only my own experience. I'm sure others know this. Especially women.

A myth has developed about women's closeness, women's bonds, women's friendships, and it has covered up our hostility to each other, and our mean-spiritedness.

Women will be supportive to each other in certain situations. We will commiserate over a miserable love affair. We'll be sympathetic about illness and other ailments. We'll swap child-rearing tips and diet aids. But we won't share anything that might help to put another female ahead of us.

Why aren't we generous to each other? Is there so little of the pie available that we have to ferociously protect our small slice? We don't share work connections and contacts. We do as little as possible to further a fellow female's career. We are not generous about anything that might enhance another woman.

Why is this? We are supposed to be the softer, gentler, more caring sex. Why are we so careless about each other? It is very disturbing.

Men don't act this way. Men understand that it is in their own interests to help other men. Even if they hate them.

We women are our own worst enemy. We continue the conflict, the bitchiness, the rivalry, the competition. And we don't see the consequences.

The consequences are clear. Men remain in control. Men are still in control of almost everything.

What is wrong with us? It starts early. Mothers and daughters seem to have more volatile relationships than their male counterparts. And it continues. Schoolgirls, from the time they are very young, want to tear and claw at each other.

Do boys do this? I don't think so.

Females are supposed to be perceptive, responsive and receptive. We are supposed to be considerate and empathetic. We are supposed to be caretakers and guardians. We are supposed to be nurturers. We do nurture. We nurture men and small children. Why don't we nurture each other?

I don't know. I just know we don't. We compete instead. We are in constant competition with other women. We want to be better mothers. We want to be more-prized wives. We want to be better cooks, better housekeepers and better lovers. We want to have better figures and be better dressed. We want to outdo each other. We want to outstrip each other. We want to kill each other. Especially if the opposition is better looking.

Good-looking women are often maligned by other women. A less-attractive woman attracts less hostility from members of her own gender.

Do men behave like this? I don't think so.

I bought the same pair of shoes I'd seen on an acquaintance. I promised her I wouldn't wear them if we were both invited to the same function. Wouldn't you laugh if a man did that? You'd laugh till you cried if a man collapsed because someone else was wearing the same tie or jacket. Men like to look like each other. Why don't women?

Women prefer to remain distant. They find sharing difficult. I understand this. I have to share my hairdresser with Fergie, the Duchess of York. It's not easy. If Fergie is in town, I have to play second fiddle. She books him up for days at a time.

He adores her. I sometimes feel jealous. A couple of years ago, some jewellery of Fergie's was stolen, from her luggage, at JFK airport. When I suggested to my hairdresser, mid-haircut, that it was less than wise for Fergie to pack jewellery in her suitcase, he didn't react well.

He stopped cutting my hair and stepped back. 'Packing jewels is not her job,' he snapped. I didn't mention Fergie for months after that.

A Co-op Building

I live in a co-op building. In Manhattan, most residences are co-ops, co-operatives. A co-operative company owns the building. People own shares in the company. Shares which vary according to the size and value of their apartment.

I liked the sound of co-operative living when I first moved here. It sounded cosy and communal.

On the surface, this is true. Things seem smooth and co-operative. A civility is maintained, on a daily basis. People say good morning and good evening and sometimes exchange other greetings. No one steals anyone else's newspapers, and most people are willing to sign for the delivery of a parcel if a neighbour is absent.

At meetings of the co-op, however, things can come unstuck. Can become not quite as civil. The most petty of grievances can be aired. There are unpleasant exchanges and unfair accusations. Strands of racism and bigotry frequently put in an appearance.

The people in my building are middle class. Artists, writers, scientists, bankers, businessmen and business-women. Individual popularity in the building rises and plummets. One minute you're in, the next moment you're out. The cause of the shift in status is usually unclear. The changing alliances and inexplicable rifts remind me of being a schoolgirl.

My husband and I had our fall from grace. Before then, I think we were reasonably well liked in the build-ing. It was more of a crash than a fall, actually.

Two-and-a-half years ago, we let our apartment for two months. Letting your apartment is a common prac-tice in New York, a city that commands exorbitant rentals.

I was persuaded to do this by a friend who rents out her town house every summer. In sixteen years, she told me, not even a glass had been broken.

The tenants we found had impeccable references. We gave the co-op board their share of the rental money, and left for Mexico. The idea was to paint – my husband is a painter – and write, in the sun, for two months dur-ing the New York winter.

While we were away, our home was burnt out. Over fifty per cent of the apartment was destroyed by fire. The Fire Marshall of New York City called us in Mexico. He was very nice. The cause of the fire, it was thought, was a faulty surge bar brought in by the tenants. Surge bars are supposed to cut out if they are overloaded. This one didn't.

I woke up in Mexico, the morning after I heard the news, and wondered if I still possessed a photograph of my late mother.

The toll was soon evident. Over a thousand of my

husband's paintings had been destroyed. Thirty years of my diaries were gone. And so were my children's child-hood photographs. And the photographs of my mother.

We came home to a mound of buckled and blackened rubble that used to be home. Fragments of years of photographs poked through the rubble. I'd been a zealous photographer and documenter of my children's lives. Both of my parents, separately, survived Auschwitz. We had no photographs or documents of their previous lives. No past we could lay our hands on.

I saw one of my mother's kitchen utensils, melted, in my kitchen and I wept.

The first thing the co-op did was ask my husband to resign from the board. The fire had grossly incon-venienced the building, they said. This was true. Smoke had entered other apartments. Someone's windows had been broken. The pungent stench of fire loitered and lingered in the building. The elevator was out of action for days.

Neighbours glared at us. A sense of neighbourliness was not really prevalent. No one offered us a coat or a cup of tea. It took us a year to rebuild and get back into our apartment. It seemed interminable.

We're back now. And the civility has reappeared. In the building people nod and say good morning and good evening.

Smell

The newest bakery to open in SoHo is Le Pain Quotidien, on Grand Street. The Vesuvio Bakery, on Prince Street, is the oldest in the area. Its exterior has been filmed in dozens of New York movies and appears on postcards and as a backdrop to fashion shots.

The Vesuvio used to be the sole bakery in the area. All of a sudden, the streets are now crowded with bakeries. Some of the city's top restaurants, like Balthazar, the Blue Ribbon and Bouley, have opened their own bakeries.

I'm not sure why bread is so suddenly chic. But the smell of all that bread being baked drives me crazy. I can't walk for two blocks in any direction from my apartment without being demented by the aroma of bread. I sometimes think they pipe the baking scents and fragrances directly from the ovens to the street. To lure you in.

Smell can be so seductive. It can transport you. To other times and other places.

The smell of newly made cardboard takes me back to my childhood. There was a cardboard factory a few doors from where we lived, as refugees, in Melbourne. I loved the smell of the cardboard. I spent endless hours watching the cardboard being cut and stacked. It was a respite from other, more difficult, aspects of my childhood.

I coveted the cardboard pieces. I still lust after cardboard. Well, I find almost any item of stationery highly desirable. In old-fashioned office-supplies stores, I am made ludicrously happy by the smell of paper and inks.

Smell is such an idiosyncratic and subjective sensation. Why does one person smell so good to us, and another person smell so repulsive? It's not easy to explain. But smell can clearly seduce and repel.

The smell of some of the streets of New York, in hot weather, is something I dread each summer. Even early in the morning, the sidewalk outside some New York restaurants has a toxic stench.

It comes from spilt garbage that has been carried out at night to wait for the garbage collection. The sidewalks are generally hosed down when the restaurant opens again the next day. In the meantime, if you walk by on an empty stomach the smell can make you retch.

Smell is a powerful asset. It plays an important role in our daily lives and in our memories. The smell of certain foods can bring back some of my food neuroses. I can relive so many difficult food moments. Moments of wanting more, wanting less, and wanting someone else's portion.

Other smells deliver better memories. Like the smell of good coffee. The aroma of freshly ground coffee is redolent of so many other things for me. Other coffees, other cafes, other conversations.

Some smells are just too alluring. Like the smell of chocolate. I have to walk past chocolate counters quickly before the smell can reach me.

Smell can also revive unpleasant associations and experiences. Like the smell of doctors' waiting rooms or the smell of dentists' implements.

Smell is so potent. It impinges on you as much as noise. I hate noise. Manhattan is very noisy. I find noise as polluting as smog or smoke. This morning, I passed a man who regularly stands in my street, singing. He has a Walkman attached to his ears. He sings along to whatever it is he is listening to.

He can't hear himself sing. Which is just as well. He is a terrible singer. His singing usually gives me a headache. This morning he was singing to Cher's hit song, 'Believe'. I recognised the tune despite his tuneless rendition.

I started thinking about Cher and felt happy. The thought that a menopausal woman could be so successful and powerful and beautiful made me want to start skipping.

I strode past the new bakery on Grand Street and didn't give the aroma of fresh *pain au chocolat* a second thought.

Presents

A friend recently gave me a pair of bright pink sheets. They were so bright they were almost fluorescent. Any brighter than this and you would need to wear dark glasses in bed.

My friend was thanking me for a favour I'd done her. My first glimpse of the sheets as they came out of the giftwrapping gave me a headache. Sleeping on sheets like these would give me a migraine. I wondered, briefly, if I looked like a person who liked to sleep on bright pink. I didn't think so.

'If you don't like them, just tell me because I love them. I really wanted to keep them for myself,' my friend said.

'They're wonderful, they'll look great on my bed,' I said.

'I thought so,' she said, sounding pleased.

Why would she think that, I thought? I've had white-on-white-on-white bedding for years. It was a big moment for me, last month, when I bought a grey blanket.

Why did I lie to my friend? Why couldn't I admit I didn't like pink sheets? After all, she'd made it easy for me. She had said she really wanted them herself. I think I was fearful that my lack of enthusiasm for the gift might strain the friendship.

I gave the sheets to the Salvation Army thrift store. And apologised for the colour. 'This colour will be very popular,' the woman there said.

I left the store thinking what a snob I was. I should be able to sleep in any colour sheets. And I should be able to tell the truth when I was given a gift. I walked down Fifth Avenue feeling bad. I was a snob and a liar. Why was it so hard for me to tell the truth?

A friend gave me a floral patterned scarf once. I was bewildered by the present. I thought it was easy to detect, from my mostly black wardrobe, that I was not really a floral person. Besides which, I never wear scarves. As soon as I put on a scarf, something happens. My appearance changes. I transmogrify into a flight attendant.

But rather than speak up, I said I loved the scarf. It is still at the back of one of my drawers.

I don't know why we can't let people know how we feel. I don't know why we can't speak to each other more honestly. But it is clear that we can't.

We have trouble saying things that would make others feel good, let alone things that would offend or cause discomfort. 'I like you so much', is hard to say. 'I want to be friends', gets stuck in your mouth once you're over ten years old.

Age doesn't make you any bolder or braver in these

matters. I still can't tell people when they've hurt my feelings. I can barely tell my grown children.

I've said yes to dinners I didn't want to go to. I've attended cocktail parties I've detested. Because I've been unable to be truthful.

I sat through *Das Rheingold*, part one of Wagner's four part opera, *Der Ring des Nibelungen*. I sat in a box at the Metropolitan Opera's production at the Lincoln Center, and pretended I was glad to be there. I'd been invited by opera lovers and couldn't admit to not wanting the invitation. Someone else might have found *Das Rheingold* exciting. But Wagner makes me tense and anxious.

I gripped the sides of my seat as Nibelungen ran around digging and working, in their underground home. I wanted to leave at the end of the second scene, but I couldn't let anyone know how I was feeling.

I was so glad when the opera ended. 'Thank you so much,' I gushed to my hosts, a married couple, on the way out of the theatre.

'Would you like to see part two, *Die Walküre*?' the man said to me.

My heart sank. I looked at him. 'Oh, yes,' I replied.

Excellent

I'm worried by cheerful people. Some people are relentlessly cheerful. They frighten me. It's unnatural to be that cheerful. I don't mind occasionally cheerful. Part-time cheerfulness pleases me. But perpetually cheerful presents a problem. And exhausts me.

I find myself getting flatter and flatter with overly cheerful people. I find myself wondering, what is behind all that cheerfulness? What is being hidden?

I empathise with people who have anxieties, complexities and difficulties more easily than I empathise with people who seem too happy. The only excessively cheerful dispositions I can tolerate belong to hospital staff and airline crews.

I'm grateful for cheerfulness in hospitals and clinics. When I've undergone X-rays or examinations or other procedures, I've scrutinised the expressions of the doctors and technicians. If they've looked bright and breezy, I've felt instantly better.

It's the same on planes. If a plane experiences turbulence or unexplained bumps or noises, I immediately examine the faces of the flight attendants. If they look cheerful, I relax.

Cheerfulness can definitely be handy. In New York you come across so many people, it's often beneficial to be cheerfully brief. To say 'Hello' with a beam. And not stop for a prolonged exchange.

I didn't understand this when I first moved here. I thought friendships and relationships flourished like they do in other places. I made the mistake of trying to be friendly, close.

I stopped and asked a neighbour how she was. She was picking up mail from the mailbox in the vestibule. 'I've had a hard week, my father's not well,' she said. She talked for over ten minutes about her elderly parents. They were ninety-eight. Both of them.

I listened to the details of her father's illness. I know how worrying it is to have an unwell parent. I marvelled, aloud, at her parents' longevity. She talked about dreading their death. I understood, I said, how hard it is to lose a parent.

I was late for an appointment, but I kept listening. She talked about having to face her own mortality when one of them died. I tried to look sympathetic. I felt she was old enough to have had many mortal thoughts.

Eventually, the conversation about her parents ended. 'And how are you?' she said to me.

'I've been a bit fragile,' I replied. I had. It had been a long, cold winter. Too long.

I'd barely finished the sentence, when her hand shot out. Like a cop stopping traffic. Her spread-eagled fingers were inches from my face. 'To be continued!' she said. 'I'm running late,' she called back to me as she left the building.

I stood in the vestibule in a daze for quite a while before I started laughing. I avoided her after that. If she was collecting her mail, I left mine in the mailbox.

There was someone else I would have liked to avoid, in another building. The first building we lived in in New York. He was the doorman. I couldn't avoid him.

He greeted the residents every time they appeared. If you asked how he was, he replied, 'Excellent'. Every time. 'Excellent', he barked, to every inquiry and every greeting. He barked it out like a sergeant major.

It always took me by surprise. Excellent seemed so overstated. And even more pronounced in New York where too many things intrude to allow anyone to feel excellent for too long. He didn't look excellent. He looked tired and alcoholic.

In the end, I admired his insistence on excellence. I've never been able to say I was excellent. I tried it once. The word got stuck in my gullet. I can't even say, 'Very good' to the question, 'How are you?'. In case 'Very good' should invoke some evil spirit. This doesn't make sense. I don't believe in spirits. 'Not bad', I used to answer. Until, after years of analysis, I progressed to 'Good'. And good is not bad. Not bad at all.

The Hamptons

The Hamptons, where wealthy New Yorkers and LA celebrities summer, is undergoing a change in topography.

The rich are moving in tonnes of earth and earth-moving equipment. This year's status symbol is a hill. Or several of them. The rich are building hills and hillocks and dunes on their properties at a furious pace.

They are sculpting and modelling elevations and undulations in what used to be flat, potato farm country.

The extra rich are adding an escarpment or two in the garden, and ponds or lakes.

The *New York Times* quoted a Hamptons real-estate broker who explained that in the sixties the outdoor barbecue pit was the essential accoutrement, in the seventies it was a swimming pool, in the eighties a tennis court and in the nineties a full-size basketball court. And now it is the ability to build hills. And to lower your tennis court. At least six feet below ground level. Why? The broker explained that this way you eliminate the noise of the bounce.

I can understand being irritated by the sound of tennis balls. But it must be tiring to be able to shape and mould your life so precisely. To be able to lift and lower the landscape and the skyline. To be able to adjust all noise levels. And play underground tennis. It would exhaust me.

With all of the fluctuation in fashion statements, how would you know you were in your own garden? One minute you could think you were on a ranch in Wyoming. You could be stoking a lamb or two on your barbecue pit, wearing cowboy boots.

And before you blinked, you could be strolling through landscape that resembles an estate in the Lake District in England. You'd have to buy a pipe and a smoking jacket. It would be so confusing.

But this lifestyle must appeal to a lot of people. A lot of celebrities. Steven Spielberg, Tom Hanks, Barbra Streisand, among others, spend their summers in the Hamptons.

I go to the Un-Hamptons. To Shelter Island. Shelter Island is off the North Fork of Long Island. The Hamptons are on the South Fork. A five-minute ferry ride separates the two places.

They are separated by more than those five minutes. The two locations could be on separate planets.

Shelter Island has no cinema, no health clubs, no spas, no boutiques, no restaurants where it is impossible to get bookings. People are not networking at picnics, on the beach. They are not shouting into a cellular phone as they watch a breathtaking sunset.

On Shelter Island, there is no need to be colour co-ordinated and coiffeured before breakfast. You can look terrible. Shelter Island attracts quiet types, and few celebrities.

The summer before last, I was driving along a small beach on Shelter Island when I thought I passed my friend Richard Plepler on a bicycle. I turned the car around and drove back towards Richard. He was bare-chested and tanned on his bicycle. I drove up and waved, but Richard looked away.

I was confused. I didn't think I'd done anything to offend him. Maybe he was having a bad day, I thought. He didn't look quite himself. Maybe it wasn't Richard?

I did another loop of the beach, and passed him again. He still didn't wave. In fact he pedalled faster. I drove back again. And stared at Richard. His bicycle wobbled dangerously.

I grinned in what I thought was a friendly manner. Richard Plepler looked terrified. He turned his bike in the other direction and pedalled furiously.

I felt hurt. And then it hit me. This was not Richard Plepler. This familiar young man was John F. Kennedy jnr. I felt terrible. I must have looked like a stalker to JFK jnr. I knew he'd never believe I thought he was Richard Plepler.

Later that day someone asked me if I'd heard that JFK jnr was on the island. I winced. I said I wish I'd heard sooner.

Hypochondria

A friend of mine was rushed to New York Hospital with appendicitis. As soon as I heard the news, I developed pains in the right side of my abdomen.

I panicked. Until I remembered I'd had my appendix removed, years ago.

I get other people's aches and twinges. I get their inflammations and itches and spasms. I'm so suggestible, I can pick up other people's lisps. I can lisp for half an hour after I've been talking to a lisper. I could probably catch vertigo or epilepsy.

I have had every symptom my husband has ever experienced. He had a ganglion removed from his leg one year. I looked so unwell while they were operating on him, the hospital offered me a bed. I limped for weeks after the operation.

I can't hear about an illness without imagining it. I'm one of those people who reads all the possible side effects listed on medication labels. I experience three quarters of them.

When someone dies, I always inquire about the cause of their death. Then I try to find out how the illness presented itself.

I subscribe to several medical newsletters. They always contain an upsetting statistic or news of an illness we should all be tested for. I can't read these newsletters at night. If I do, I can't sleep.

I'm not alone in being suggestible. I read that scientists consistently find that thirty to forty per cent of all patients given a placebo show improvements for a wide variety of conditions. From seasickness to migraine, angina and post-operative pain.

And ten per cent of people taking a placebo report side effects normally associated with a chemically active drug.

I own a shelf of books about health. I own medical encyclopedias. Owning these books reassures me.

A friend rang me one night. He was upset. His wife's temperature was up. She had the flu. At what point, he wondered, should he take her to a hospital?

It is worrying to be unwell in New York. Most of us don't have a family doctor we know well. And certainly not one we can call at night.

I consulted my library. I looked under fever. I got waylaid by glaucoma, hearing loss and stroke risk before I learned that for adults, a temperature of over 103 or 104 degrees Fahrenheit was cause for concern.

After that, I was up all night trying not to think about going deaf or becoming a stroke victim.

I wish I wasn't so anxious. Earlier this year, I read about a psychiatrist in California who created anxious mice in the hope of understanding more about human anxiety.

This scientist bred his mice to be nervous. He blocked out one of a group of genes called serotonin receptors. It worked. His mice were skittish, nervous and reticent. They startled easily. In new situations they froze and hugged the nearest wall.

I identified with those edgy, indecisive, highly strung mice. I'm easily upset. A poster, which used to be prominently displayed in all New York restaurants, used to upset me. The poster demonstrated the Heimlich manoeuvre. A manoeuvre designed to help people who are choking. It used to take away my appetite. I'd spend half the meal wondering what to do if I saw someone choking.

There is always something to worry about. Last spring was a particularly bad season for hay fever sufferers. The pollen count in New York was continually high.

I read that it was a good idea for hay fever sufferers to wash their hair at night after being outside. This prevented pollen from falling on the pillow and causing night-time sneezing.

I began to wash my hair at night. My husband fell about laughing. 'You've never had hay fever,' he said.

'It's a preventative measure,' I answered.

Day Spas

Day spas are all the rage in New York. So many have opened in the last year or two.

There are three or four within walking distance of where I live in SoHo. The very newest, the Helena Rubinstein Beauty Gallery, is on the site of two former art galleries. No one can afford to sell art in SoHo anymore. The rentals are too expensive.

What is a day spa? For a start, it's a place to spend money. Lots of it. You go to a spa to recuperate and recover from the rest of your life.

The Helena Rubinstein spa offers firming and sculpting facials. You can also have facials for your back. 'You'll be ready for anything backless or strapless,' the store's brochure tells you.

You can have a sugar scrub, to 'take sugar's revitalising qualities to new heights'. I know how revitalising sugar can be. Two pieces of Lindt bittersweet chocolate and I am euphoric.

Because this is New York, the Helena Rubinstein spa offers an express facial. It takes just thirty minutes.

Spas serve a purpose. You go to a spa to feel pampered and indulged. To have your pores and your psyche unclogged. To have your epidermis and your nervous system stroked and massaged and powdered. To have your spirit exfoliated and invigorated.

You go there for the pleasure of it. That's if you like that sort of thing. I don't. Spas make me tense.

I'm suspicious of what they are selling. I suspect that you leave with little more than a lot of attention. I prefer to get my attention in other ways. I've had three analysts over a twenty-year period.

Mud packs and cellulite wraps make me claustrophobic. In order to have a relaxing massage, I need to be intravenously injected with Valium.

I feel faintly inadequate for not being able to experience the spa bliss that others seem to. I sometimes feel I'm a spa failure.

I once took my younger daughter to a spa with me. I thought I might feel better there if I had company. I booked us both in for a massage. My daughter was nearly asleep before they touched her. I was so tense, I wondered if I had a beta-blocker in my bag to lower my blood pressure.

The masseuse kept telling me to relax. I'm trying, I kept saying to her. She massaged and smoothed and kneaded. I was so anxious my breathing became irregular and uneven.

'Close your eyes,' the masseuse said when she reached my face.

'I can't,' I said. 'I need to keep them open.' I could hear her jaw clenching.

I was so happy when the massage was over. I planned to shower as soon as I got home. I couldn't wait to wash off the strange scents and aromas that had been rubbed into me.

On the way out, I noticed that the other customers looked blissed out, dreamy. My younger daughter appeared comatose.

It took me two hours after I left the spa for my breathing to return to its regular pattern. And my face felt tight and itchy. That night, I looked in the mirror. My normally clear complexion was blotched. I looked a wreck.

My daughter rang to see if I'd calmed down. 'I'm never doing that again,' I said to her. And I'm not.

The only beauty parlour I feel comfortable in is Olga's, on La Guardia Place. I go there for pedicures. All the pedicurists and manicurists and beauticians are Russian.

They are warm and effusive and overexcitable. They panic easily, over small things. Like a missing pencil or a misplaced nail polish.

I love them. I love listening to their exchanges in Russian. It all sounds imperative and urgent. The arguments and questions and concerns that fly between them remove my tension. I become calm in their presence. Ten minutes at Olga's and I'm a new person.

Children

In the last year, four bright young women I know have left their jobs to have children.

I felt bothered by this. Worried. Flat. I felt a sense of loss. These women had departed for an unknown destination. Motherhood. I wasn't sure that any of them would come back.

I had implored each of them not to leave. Have the baby, I said, but don't stay away for too long. Come back soon.

I felt as though they were moving to Mars. And motherhood, in a way, resembles life on another planet. A planet where milk formulas and teething gel take precedence over what is happening in Kosovo or anywhere else.

I had talked to one of the young women, an editor, for hours. I talked to her about not losing herself. Not substituting a child's achievements for her own.

Then she left. And I felt she was lost to me. Gone. I

felt she'd landed in another universe. The universe of motherhood. This universe scoops up and swallows its occupants.

And unlike Dorothy who was whisked off in *The Wizard of Oz*, the mothers are not back in Kansas when they wake up. They are still in motherhood territory. And it is so easy to be lost there. I know. I was lost for years.

I had my children when I was very young. I remember those years as lonely and depressing, although I don't think depression was what I felt at the time.

I was too busy. Too busy busying myself. I cleaned the house. I perfected a perfect cheesecake. And baked hundreds of them.

I visited playgrounds, and took regular trips to the fire station to admire the fire engines, with small children. I assembled and disassembled jigsaw puzzles and pieces of Lego. Pretty soon my brain was in pieces.

My cleverness was submerged in diapers, pacifiers and pureed pumpkin. Pieces of dried pumpkin were stuck to the sleeves of all of my clothes. My brain had become pumpkin pulp.

I've watched too many women bury their brains. I've watched too many women bury themselves in husbands and children. They lose all of their abilities except the ability to clean up after others.

Men don't do this. Men don't discard their brains when they become parents. It is easier for men. No one expects them to stay home with children. This is still felt to be a woman's role.

Society, still, in this enlightened age, looks askance, or with pity, at women who choose careers over children. And admires women who give up their jobs for their children.

Motherhood is a thankless job. Children never remember what you did for them. What they never forget is what you failed to do.

My elder daughter has said that I never drove her to parties. All the other mothers drove their daughters, she said. My strongest memories of those years are of driving children. To parties, to ballet classes and drama lessons. Driving them to tae kwon do and piano teachers. Driving them to their friends' houses. Driving them to school and back. I was always in the car. Driving myself crazy.

My children, who are now adults, have also voiced complaints about their lack of religious guidance. Religion played almost no part in their upbringing. I thought I was giving them a choice, a freedom. They saw it as an omission.

'I took you to a few synagogues and churches,' I said to my younger daughter.

'That's because you liked the buildings,' she said. She was right.

I've always been drawn to religious buildings. To churches, synagogues and mosques. They seem to be places where the more superficial aspects of life fall away. They seem to contain a peacefulness. A peacefulness that is hard to obtain in other places. A peacefulness that can be almost elusive when you are a parent.

Dress Size

'You'd be a size four,' the shop assistant in SoHo says to me when I ask if I can try on the navy light-weight coat in the window.

'No way,' I say to her. 'I'm quite big.'

I am. For a start I am five feet nine. I have thirty-nine-and-a-half inch hips. No one has ever suggested that I am a size four. Size four is a size six in Australia and a size thirty-six in Germany. Size four is petite.

'I'm quite big,' I say again.

'No you're not,' she says.

'Yes I am,' I say.

'You're slim,' she says.

'I'm not a size four,' I say. I pat my hips for emphasis. She looks down at my hips. They are not hard to find. I pat them again.

'I'll bring you a size six,' she says.

I watch her walk towards the rack of coats. I realise I'm torn between a disbelief at the thought that anyone could take me for a size four and a hovering hope that maybe I really am that slim.

I stand up straight, and suck in my stomach so that it's flat. I feel myself flush with pleasure at the thought of how thin I must look.

When I can't get my arms into the sleeves of the coat, the shop assistant shakes her head. 'It's cut small,' she says.

I feel exhausted. Earlier, in another store, a salesman has insisted that I am an extra small. Headless and limbless, I would still not be an extra small.

I hate shopping, anyway. I always seem to look ugly in clothing stores. I usually try to avoid looking in the mirror when I try clothes on. An action that seems at odds with my mission.

I end up with a size ten coat. It fits. On the way home, I think I've spotted a new trend. Sales assistants in New York, I decide, are being encouraged to make the customer feel thin. This is not a good thing.

Women suffer enough over their size and their looks. In America, eight-year-old girls are already dieting. And no woman I know, regardless of age, feels altogether happy about her appearance.

I can try on four outfits before deciding what to wear for the evening. If my husband kept changing his shirts and trousers before he could leave the house, I'd be completely bewildered. Or dissolved in hysterical fits of laughter.

My husband has never asked me if a colour suits him, or if the cut of a shirt makes him look fat. Both questions I've asked about various clothes I own, more than once.

I relate the ordeal to my eighty-four-year-old father when he calls me from Australia, where he lives. 'It's ridiculous to call me thin,' I say to him. 'But I have lost some weight. As a matter of fact, I weigh less than I did when I was twelve.'

'That's because you was always such a big type,' he says. 'You was a stocky, stubby girl.'

I don't like his choice of words. I feel hurt. I decide it is his English. My father, a Polish-Jewish refugee to Australia, has never really mastered some of the subtleties of the language.

'I wasn't stocky,' I answer. 'I never had broad shoulders.'

'It's not necessary to have broad shoulders to be stocky,' he tells me. He sighs. 'Why are we talking about this?' he says. 'I rang to say that I miss you and I love you. When are you coming to Australia?'

'I wasn't stocky,' I repeat. 'And I wasn't stubby. I was always tall. You can't be stubby and tall.'

'You was stubby and chunky,' he replies. I am reminded that tact has never been one of my father's strong points.

'What are you arguing with me for?' my father says. 'You was fat.'

'Okay, I was fat,' I say. 'But I'm not fat now.'

'That is true,' he says.

Well, I'm not fat. But I'm not thin. And I'm not a size four.

Noise

Now that muggers have been replaced by Prada stores and friendly policemen in New York, visitors to the city, it seems, are worrying about the decibel levels attacking their ears.

In the last few weeks, half a dozen people, all visitors, have mentioned to me how tiring, agitating and debilitating New York's noise is. They are right. New York is an extremely noisy city. And the noise can drive you nuts. It never stops.

I've tried to find the pre-dawn clanging and banging of the trash collection trucks reassuring. To view them as ushering in a fresh, newly cleaned day.

But many of the other omnipresent noises still startle and disturb me. The jackhammers, for instance. There is always a road or a sidewalk being dug up. No matter what part of the city you live in, a road works crew will be working in the vicinity.

Teams of men will be drilling and grinding and digging

and excavating, and mixing and pouring in a street near you. They'll be uprooting and replacing cobblestones and curbs and any asphalt surface.

Every avenue and street appears to be under continual construction. The city streets should be as smooth and seamless as Carrara marble. But they're not.

For a few weeks, the newly repaired street looks new. And then the cracks and the potholes reappear. And the street looks exactly like it used to. And the road crews are called in.

The short life span of the street repairs must have something to do with the volume of traffic in New York. The *New York Times*, in an article on the paucity of parking space in the city, pointed out that 934,000 cars come onto Manhattan each morning.

The wear and tear of all those vehicles and all those people must be immense. The 934,000 cars, the newspaper said, compete for 127,000 spaces in parking garages.

This could account for some of the frayed nerves and bad tempers of some of the drivers. Their honking and tooting makes up what is instantly recognisable as a New York soundtrack. The sound of car horns.

It would be impossible to find a street in Manhattan that isn't resounding with the sound of car horns. Day and night. It is almost a prerequisite for driving in this city that you turn into an impatient, hostile, and often foul-mouthed, maniac the minute you get behind the wheel of a car.

I hate all that jarring blasting and honking.

Except when I get into a New York taxi. And then I turn into a lunatic. If the traffic is slow, I want the driver to toot at everything. If he just sits there, I get anxious.

I think he doesn't care about the meter climbing and the time passing. If he beeps and beeps, I know it matters.

I used to use a Russian car service here. The cars were shabby and often stank of stale cigarettes, but the drivers were reliable. If something held them up, they would toot incessantly and grimace and mutter and curse in Russian. It always relaxed me.

There are other noises, too. Large trucks thunder through the streets. And there is always an ambulance or a police car or a fire truck trying to get somewhere fast.

In the middle of all this abundance of aural assault are Americans themselves. They are very noisy. They speak loudly and forcefully wherever they are. They are noisy and blunt.

A friend from Düsseldorf told me about an encounter he'd had with a woman who was trying to pick him up in a chic bar on the Upper East Side. He was really offended by what seemed just a bit of New York bluntness to me.

'How can you possibly live in Düsseldorf?' she'd said to him.

'Düsseldorf is a sophisticated, cultured city,' he said to me, still looking pained.

I nodded. I like Düsseldorf.

'Düsseldorf is a vibrant, exciting city,' he said in a peeved voice.

I looked at him. 'In Düsseldorf,' I said, 'you can hear the sound of your own footsteps.'

He looked dismayed.

Food

I visited a friend who lives in upstate New York. She lives next door to a dairy farm. I arrived at her house at night.

I stepped out of the house in the morning and saw cows being milked. I went into a state of hyperexcitement. And astonishment. I couldn't believe that cows still had to be milked. I thought that by now cows must surely be obsolete. I thought that milk must be manufactured in plants and factories.

To see cows walking around in a field, like cows are supposed to, was quite startling. The cows were not in pens, or hooked up or wired to high-tech equipment. They looked like cows do in picture books.

I stood and stared at the cows. My first thought was that these cows had been brought here for a movie shoot. SoHo, where I live, is awash with film crews. I thought that the cows must have been providing a bucolic backdrop for somebody's story.

Then I realised that the cows belonged to the dairy farm. It was a shocking realisation. It was hard to take in the fact that the cows were being milked for milk.

I think I'd assumed that, in this modern age, milk was made already encased in cartons. It made me think that eggs must still come from hens. All the hens I've had contact with have been wrapped in plastic. It's been years since I've seen a live hen, let alone seen one in the vicinity of an egg.

I'm clearly a bit removed from nature and natural occurrences. I don't mind this distance, really. Too much harmony with the earth can be bothersome.

Once I almost broke a tooth on a large piece of grit hidden in a home-grown celery stalk. I could still feel granules of dirt in my mouth for hours after I'd finished the celery salad.

Vegetables in produce stores impress me. I'm full of admiration for produce set out on shelves. A display of plump strawberries in a fruit shop can completely uplift me, while strawberries that are still attached to the earth don't seem that appetising.

I don't even know how most fruits and vegetables are grown. I've never seen a cherry tree. Or a brussel sprout still connected to its branch. I think that today, most people haven't.

Soon, just as you visit a zoo to view certain species of birds and animals, you'll have to go to museums to learn about food and its origins.

Instead of reconstructing the natural habitat of lions and giraffes and tigers, like zoos, these museums will mount exhibitions of food. They'll build fields and groves to show us where bananas and potatoes come from.

In New York, and most big cities, our fruit and vegetables are often airfreighted to us. We eat tomatoes from California and grapes from Israel and mangoes from Mexico.

Our food is labelled and tagged. Everything comes with its own sticker. Each individual pear, plum and pumpkin carries its own biography. Its own ID.

Sometimes they speak to you. *Hi, I'm an acorn squash and I was grown in Oklahoma*, a squash I bought last week said. I felt I should greet the squash with, 'Pleased to meet you.'

I'm a vine-ripened tomato grown in New Jersey, was the message on my tomato. I half expected the tag on the tomato to contain the name and place of birth of the tomato's parents. Like adoption papers.

The last mango I bought had *Mango* printed on a large sticker across the top of the fruit. I couldn't see the point of this. Was it in case I thought I was buying an octopus or a side of beef?

Most of us can still identify the food we eat even though we haven't grown it ourselves. A woman in our building brought in some lettuces she'd grown at her country home. The whole building was agog at her achievement. 'Isn't she clever?' person after person said. You'd have thought she'd just won the Nobel Prize for literature or nuclear physics.

Leopard-skin Trousers

L ast winter, I bought my husband a pair of narrow-legged, velvet leopard-skin-print trousers. They were a bargain. Reduced to half price. The fifty per cent discount made the trousers irresistible.

I'm not sure why the leopard skin so instantly appealed to me. But it did. When I held the trousers up, I felt happy. They looked joyful and carefree. Well, as carefree as it is possible for an inanimate object to look.

I think the wild yellow and orange and black and brown spots appealed to my more flamboyant, more extroverted inclinations. Inclinations I keep hidden. From myself. I don't have easy access to my more unrestrained tendencies.

I took the trousers home, carefully giftwrapped. My husband hated them. That is not strictly true. At first they made him laugh. That was before he found out that I'd bought them for him.

'I'm sure they'll look fabulous on you,' I said. He

shook his head and looked perplexed. 'They were half price,' I said. 'And non refundable.' He didn't answer. He walked quietly into his studio.

I knew I had made a mistake. I resolved, right there and then, that I would avoid all sales in the future.

New York has stupendous sales. Twice a year. In summer and in winter. Everything that can be bought and sold is on sale. Every department store and small shop discounts their merchandise. Items that are impossibly priced for the rest of the year are available for a relatively modest outlay. You can be Dolce & Gabbana'd up to your eyebrows. You can wear Yves St Laurent hats and Christian La Croix socks if you can find them.

The morning after my leopard-skin pants purchase, I was working in my study when my husband appeared. He was wearing the trousers. The sight of the trousers obliterated all else from my head. They looked shocking. They had turned my husband into a 1960s remnant, stuck in a time warp, or a character who had inadvertently wandered out of the third act of an opera.

I forgot what I was writing about. I just stared at my husband. The trousers were so loud, so gaudy, so garish. What had I been thinking?

My husband said he was about to go out. 'You are not going to go out wearing those trousers, are you?' I said.

'You didn't buy them for me to wear around the house, did you?' he asked me.

I didn't answer. I was still dumbstruck. 'I'm going to pretend I'm Elton John or Rod Stewart,' he said, and left.

I felt depressed. And worried about what the neighbours would think. I knew it was my own doing. Why had I done this? What on earth had possessed me to buy those trousers?

Something takes over my brain when I see a sales sign. I go haywire. I have disregarded size, colour and style. If an item is a quarter of its price, I have bought it.

I have bought dresses that didn't fit, in the hope that they would stretch. They never did. I have bought garments with a twist in the shoulder or sleeve that never untwisted. I've bought shirts with collars that weren't quite right, but were cheap. I bought a bright green coat once. It made me look seasick.

You'd think I'd have learned from these previous mistakes and miscalculations and money-saving ventures. You'd think I would never have been swept off my feet by leopard-skin trousers.

If only I hadn't been. My husband, who grew up in poverty, is a man who cannot bear to waste an item of clothing. I knew I'd be seeing those trousers for a long time. And I was right. They've been curiously sturdy and resilient. My husband seems to have had them on constantly. I think he grew quite fond of them. I never did. They made me edgy.

Last month the knees wore out. I rejoiced. I was never meant to be married to Elton John or Rod Stewart.

Lies

I read, in the *New York Times*, that you can now buy telephones that are able to detect lies.

There is a phone that can pick up changes that take place in a caller's voice if they are lying. This phone costs $3,900.

A cheaper phone is available. This phone can detect suspicious dips and rises in the voices of callers. For only $129.

These phones bother me. I'm not sure it's a good idea to uncover untruths. Some untruths are essential. For example compliments that are not entirely accurate. And other forms of kindness or flattery.

Sometimes it doesn't make sense to tell the truth. Sometimes it would be just plain stupid.

I don't like dogs. Every now and then the odd dog captures my imagination. But, on the whole, I don't like dogs. I keep quiet about this. I don't broadcast my dislike of dogs. I feel faintly inadequate for not being a dog lover.

I've pretended to be a dog lover, to dog-loving people, on more than one occasion. People are suspicious of those who don't like dogs.

Sometimes the judgmental attitudes of dog lovers prove too much for me. I explain my aversion to dogs as an allergy. People are sympathetic about allergies.

Dogs don't know I don't like them. They always rush to me, looking cheerful. They lick me. They sniff me. They look at me adoringly. They can't tell I don't like them.

When my children were younger, we often had a dog. A dog I had agreed to grudgingly. The children were always so happy with their dog. I was miserable. I work at home. I was stuck at home with the dog.

One of the dogs who drove me crazy was Solly. My husband and the children adored Solly. Solly ran away every day. Every day someone would call me and say that they had found Solly. And I would have to stop work and go out and get him.

A woman rang me one afternoon. 'I've got Dolly,' she said. The engraver who had engraved Solly's silver identification tag hadn't done a good job. People often called Solly Dolly.

'He's called Solly,' I said with irritation. 'Just leave him where he is.'

'I'll call the RSPCA. The Royal Society for the Prevention of Cruelty to Animals,' she said. I went out and retrieved Solly.

I fantasised about giving Solly away and saying I'd lost him. Writers are always fantasising and daydreaming. I daydreamed half of my childhood away.

I grew up with few relatives. I used to invent aunts, uncles, cousins and grandmothers and grandfathers. I spent hours making up relatives. I gave myself Buddy Holly, as a long-lost brother, when I was ten. In my fantasy, Buddy Holly would take off his glasses when he saw me and see how alike we were.

At school, I borrowed a boy's black-rimmed glasses. I tried them on in front of the bathroom mirror. To see if I looked like Buddy. The lenses were too thick for me to see anything. The truth was I didn't have a brother.

My father is fond of the truth. He was with me while I was doing an interview a few years ago. We had planned to go out to dinner after the interview.

The interview was in a cafe. I told my father it wouldn't take long. Thirty minutes at the most. My father ordered a cappuccino and looked engrossed in his coffee.

I answered the journalist's questions. I was trying to be charming. Trying to be interesting. I answered a difficult question and was relieved I'd got through the answer, when my father interrupted us. He contradicted what I'd said.

I couldn't believe it. 'It didn't happen the way you said it did,' my father said. I didn't want to start a family argument in front of the journalist. I glared at my father. He deflected my glare. 'The truth is the truth,' he declared.

A Man

In this post-feminist era, being single still holds a stigma. For women. Even in as sophisticated a city as New York, unattached women are seen as disadvantaged. Having a man confers status. Any man.

If a man is bald, overweight, unkempt and elderly, he is still considered an eligible bachelor. If he has stained teeth, and hairs protruding from his nose and ears, he can still be seen as a good catch. A woman in a similar state would be shunned.

A man can be antisocial. He can be short tempered. He can smell. And still be viewed as highly desirable. His rudeness or shyness or smell or temper can be interpreted as a charming idiosyncrasy. A rude, smelly woman would be considered a burden.

Why are men so prized? And women so underrated? I don't know.

What I do know is that men seem scarce. In Florida, where there are many retirees, if a man is still breathing he is seen as a hot property. A prospective prince charming.

And in New York, women are always bemoaning the lack of men. The streets of New York seem full of men. But the city seems overflowing with single women. Women over thirty are starting to feel desperate, over the hill.

Everyone in the city knows a good man is hard to find. 'Hang on to that man,' a homeless woman called out to me after my husband had given her five dollars.

Churches and other religious organisations are still venues for meeting people. And are increasingly popular with young New Yorkers. I suggested one of these to my younger daughter. More for the social value than for any more pious purpose. I'd read about a lecture series at an uptown synagogue. After the lecture, I'd read, the guests mingled.

My daughter had just broken up with a boyfriend. I suggested the lecture series as a diversion. A diversion, I hoped, might give her a broader view of the world. And more young men to choose from than the one she was sitting at home sobbing over.

She was reluctant to go. I said I thought it could be an intellectually interesting evening.

'Lecture series?' she said to me the next morning. 'No one even pretended they were there for the lecture.' The diversion had worked. She was fuming. 'It was a meat market,' she said. 'Guys eyed you up and down, and offered you their business card if they thought you looked good enough.'

'I'm sorry,' I said. But she hadn't finished.

'The women were all dressed and pressed and made-up to the hilt,' she fumed. 'It was not my crowd. All the guys were bankers and lawyers.'

'There's nothing that terrible about bankers and lawyers,' I said.

'Let's not get into that,' she answered.

I told a friend about my daughter's experience. 'Those things are a nightmare,' my friend said. 'You're so lucky you've got a husband.' I've been told this before in New York. Endlessly.

It's disconcerting to be continually told how lucky you are to have your husband. I've been told so many times, since I moved here, how lucky I am to have him.

I know this. My husband is a man I've been in love with for a long time. I left another man, another marriage, to be with him. Still, there's a limit to how many times I need to be reminded that I'm lucky to have him.

No one has ever suggested he's lucky to have me. Not even my father. My father admitted, when pressed, that my husband might not be as happy with someone else. A not altogether wholehearted endorsement of his daughter.

'He's lucky to have me,' I once volunteered to my father. There was a silence. As though my father was digesting my statement.

'Of course,' he said, eventually.

'Thank you,' I said sarcastically. He didn't notice the sarcasm.

'Your husband is a very good husband,' he said. 'You are very lucky to have him.'

A Cellular Phone

I was walking in the street, in Frankfurt, on my last book tour, when my cellular phone rang.

I jumped, even though I had been alert and listening, to make sure I'd hear it if it should ring.

The publicist, who was travelling with me, had given me the phone and instructions on its use. I only absorbed the 'send' and 'end' details.

She knew I was a cell-phone novice, and stressed that I had to listen for the ring. In heavy traffic, she said, it was easy to miss. And she needed to be able to get hold of me.

I set off on my walk. With my cell phone. I felt like an electronically tagged prisoner. Or a harnessed and leashed child let loose. I was so happy to be out of the hotel. Book tours can be hard work. I was happy to have been given a couple of hours to myself.

I nearly fell over in my haste to get to the phone when it rang. 'Hello,' I shouted. There was no answer. I shouted louder. 'Hello, hello.'

No one replied to me. I shouted a few more times. And then felt stupid shouting to myself in the streets of Frankfurt. I pressed 'end' and put the phone back in my backpack.

A minute later, it rang again. I almost dislocated my right shoulder pulling off my backpack. I said my name firmly into the phone. I've watched lots of business people answer like that. No one responded.

The same thing happened again a short time later. And kept happening. Ten minutes after I'd left the hotel for a break and some fresh air, my head was splitting.

I wondered if whoever was ringing me was leaving messages. I knew the phone had a voice-mail service. But of course I couldn't find it. I pressed a few buttons. A recorded voice spoke to me. It seemed to be issuing instructions. Possibly instructions on message retrieval. I couldn't tell. The voice was speaking in German.

I decided to give up on my walk. It hadn't been very relaxing. And whoever was trying to contact me clearly felt some sense of urgency. I turned back and walked in the direction of the hotel. The phone kept ringing. Halfway there, I noticed that the ringing sound seemed to be coming from above me.

That thought hit me with such force, I stopped walking. I stood on the spot, in shock.

The phone rang again. Or rather what I thought was the phone rang once more. The shrill ring that was ringing now, and had been ringing all morning, was not my phone. It was a bird whistling.

And warbling and chirping. The trills and twitters and insistent cheeping that had been dogging me had not been my cell phone. It had come from the throats of the birds of Frankfurt.

I was stunned. How could birds sound so like a cell phone? Why hadn't the phone manufacturers anticipated this problem? And why were there so many birds in Frankfurt?

I adjusted to the phone after that incident. Well almost. I nearly knocked myself out cold, in the Paris Bar in Berlin, when I slammed my bag into my head to hear if it was my phone that was ringing.

I've come a long way since then. I've almost become a cell-phone expert and a cell-phone addict. I no longer look down on people who make restaurant reservations while they are walking. I no longer sit in judgment of shoppers who call each other from different floors of the same department store. Or people who dissect their love lives at the traffic lights.

I'm a caller myself. I make all sorts of calls. Calls which are boring indoors, like arranging dental appointments, become quite exciting when made outside.

Last week I called my younger daughter to let her know which street I was walking on. She was bewildered, but tolerant.

Monica

I've been looking around, and I think I can see an unintended consequence, a side effect, of Monica Lewinsky and all that oral sex with the president.

It seems to me that more and more young women are allowing themselves to be a bit bigger. Whippet thin no longer seems to be the size of the moment.

Flat chests and concave hips are becoming less common, even among models. Young women are dressing in a way that emphasises a voluptuousness.

This past summer the streets of New York were suddenly filled with more cleavage than has been seen here for years. And this was not all. Midriffs with flesh to spare were bared. All of a sudden a little padding around the hips and the stomach was not akin to a death sentence or an admission of failure.

Rounded curves were being flaunted shamelessly. It was almost shocking. And hard to adjust to. After all we've been blitzed with the notion that thinner is better for well over a decade.

I first noticed this phenomenon at the beginning of the summer. I was having coffee at the Des Moines Cafe, in the East Village. Three young women in a row came into the cafe, separately, with partly bared torsos.

They were sporting hipster skirts and low-slung trousers and a lot of tanned skin. Two of them had navel rings. None of the women looked like Kate Moss. They were well built, curvaceous. I was almost shocked by the sight of women baring bodies that were not ultraflat. Bodies that rose and fell and dipped and curved. Women this size used to curl up in bed with thick pyjamas and a diet book.

They used to cover themselves up when they left the house. They wore flattening bras, and what were euphemistically referred to as body firmers. Girdles in plain English.

Until this year, flesh that was exposed had to be hardly there.

Over the summer, I saw more and more women of more normal proportions. Hip young women, who ten years ago would have had their rib cages protruding from under cropped T-shirts, looked healthy and strong. Women with breasts and hips.

The saying, 'You can't be too rich or too thin', might be about to disappear from our vernacular. I think Monica could be responsible for this. I think the president's choice of partner in this unfortunate liaison may have had some unexpected repercussions for women.

Monica's fuller figure was photographed and filmed endlessly. Although I was dismayed by Clinton's dalliance, I found myself feeling pleased that Monica was a larger rather than smaller young woman.

No matter how muddled and muddy Monica and Bill's relationship might have been, it was clear that Clinton found Monica's body attractive.

We have been so besieged by the image of ultrathin women as highly desirable. Monica could have been a natural corrective. I think Monica may have made it all right to have a body which moves and has life.

The bodies we've been exposed to in magazines and movies are so sparse. We've become accustomed to models and actresses who could leap over Niagara Falls without one part of their body quivering.

I should, at this point, admit to a lack of objectivity, to a bias on this subject. I've never been thin.

Maybe Monica's influence has even spread to Los Angeles. Los Angeles has always been a more superficial city than New York. Appearance is everything in LA.

The last time I went to Los Angeles, I was invited to a party. At the party I was introduced to a very pregnant actress. I love the look of a pregnant belly. I said how great she looked. She pulled up the top she was wearing. 'Look,' she said, 'all baby, no fat.'

I didn't know what to say. I contemplated hitching up my own top and grabbing some flesh to show her. 'Look, all fat, no baby,' I wanted to say. But I didn't.

Supermarket

The first time I saw an American supermarket was just after I had interviewed Janis Joplin. It was in California. I was nineteen and an Australian rock journalist.

I was so bowled over by the size of the Cornflakes packets and the volume of the ice-cream containers, that all thoughts of Janis went out of my head. I found the article hard to write. All I could think about was the supermarket.

I'm still entranced by supermarkets. I still love them. But only in certain locations. Not in big cities. I have to get my supermarket fix when I go to the country or the seaside.

In New York, it is easier and quicker to buy everything, from shoe polish to sandwiches and condoms, in delicatessens. You don't have to engage in warfare with New Yorkers wielding supermarket trolleys. You don't have to wait in line for half an hour.

Of course, in delicatessens, the choice is more limited

and the price more expensive. But the service is instant. And time is everything in this city.

This emphasis on speed and efficiency can eliminate more than time wasted. It can deprive you of ordinary, everyday things. Like washing your own clothes and shopping in supermarkets.

Activities that at first glance you might be pleased to be rid of, but a dearth of which, in the long term, can leave you bereft.

I felt ludicrously pleased recently when I hand washed a garment. The alternative was to drop the garment off at the laundry or have the laundry pick it up. Washing clothes is not something I want to do every day. But I found the experience curiously satisfying and fulfilling. It was a weird feeling for a chore to metamorphose into a pleasure.

In New York, going to the supermarket is a chore, a burden. They are always crowded and always busy. The fluorescent lighting alone puts me in a state of near nervous breakdown.

An out-of-town supermarket is another matter altogether. It is a quietly exciting adventure for me. I stroll through the aisles and browse. I buy all sorts of things I don't need and will never use. Last year I bought those little silver balls you put on cakes. I'm a terrible cake maker. But I also bought some pink cake decorating paste. In case my ability to bake cakes improves.

I've bought bright orange kitchen sponges and matching dishwashing liquid, and pretended that I live in a village, where I can wash dishes and daydream.

Washing dishes in Manhattan is merely depressing. And time consuming. Another task to be fitted in.

In a quest for efficiency in New York, one year I

decided that we'd eat from disposable cutlery and crockery. It was a bad decision. Any food that didn't have a solid grip slipped off the plastic forks. And it was impossible to cut anything denser than a banana or a piece of over-cooked pumpkin with the plastic knives.

Our meals slipped and dipped off our utensils. It was a less than sophisticated dining experience. When my children ate with us, they nearly died laughing. And then began berating us. About the environment and the damage we were unleashing with all that plastic.

After that I switched to paper cups and plates. They weren't waterproof. I had to eliminate sauces and soups from our diet. In the end I went back to ordinary dishes. And dish washing.

Dish washing needn't be dismal. I have joyful memories of my mother and her friends washing up together after dinner parties. The best part of the evening's conversation occurred during the washing and drying. You'd really hear what they thought of each other and the rest of the guests. I'd strain to catch each word.

There's something satisfying about discussing someone's awful husband or how much weight they've put on. It's strangely uplifting to be able to exchange gossip and be bitchy.

In New York, no one has time for gossip or bitchiness or dishes.

A Couple

There is a couple, a man and a woman who live in my street. Literally. They don't live in one of the smart lofts or elegant apartments. They live in the street.

They've made their home on the metal landing at the top of several steps, which leads to the back door of a hip downtown clothing store. A store so profitable that it has no need for this entrance.

It leaves unused what is considered prime street frontage. Space like this rents for between ten thousand and thirty thousand dollars a month in this area. And it is here that the couple has made a home for themselves.

The recessed doorway offers them some protection from the weather. I think that some warmth from the building's boiler, in the basement, may reach them in winter. They have been living on this landing, on and off, for over a year.

She is white and he is African American. I don't know how old they are. Homelessness is an instant ageing process. This woman could be thirty and she could be fifty.

They are often still asleep when I leave the house in the morning. They sleep side by side. Bundled up and tucked in by rags and blankets.

Sometimes, in the afternoon, I've seen the man packing their bedding up. I've seen him carefully fold worn garments and pieces of stained fabric into a supermarket trolley. The trolley is always parked right by them.

They often sit on the landing and talk, quietly, to each other. Sometimes, they stretch out on a step, toe to toe, and read newspapers.

If they didn't look so worn and battered. If they weren't living in the street. If her face and legs weren't covered with red sores and scabs, and he didn't have most of his teeth missing, you could take them for an average suburban couple.

A few weeks ago, he had a folding chair out on the sidewalk and was reading a magazine. In another life, he could have been relaxing on the patio while she prepared dinner.

They are always together. And seem so compatible. So at ease with each other. Their togetherness under these harshest of circumstances is almost overwhelming. And disturbing. It is a very loud reminder of their humanity.

In New York most of us manage to look away from the homelessness we see every day. We manage to pretend that the person sleeping in the street is not someone exactly like us.

I was disturbed by this couple from the moment I first saw them. I felt terrible walking by with my expensive groceries and fruit and vegetables. I wanted to do something. To give them some money. But I couldn't. I was too nervous to stop. Too frightened to intrude. The truth is I was probably too frightened to enter their world. Even briefly. For weeks I tried to do something. And still couldn't.

I made excuses for my behaviour. I was worried about losing my anonymity, I told myself, after all I had to pass the couple every day. I should have been more worried about my heartlessness.

I'm not alone in this ability to look away. No one who passes the couple ever pauses. No one talks to them. And I understand. For most people, this city is an edgy enough place without introducing another random element.

I passed the woman, early in the morning, recently. She was walking back to her home on the landing. Her hair looked wet, freshly washed. I was surprised. I wondered where on earth she had managed to wash her hair.

I wanted to grab my purse and hand her some money. And again, I didn't. I thought it might embarrass her.

When I got home, I realised what a middle-class supposition I was making. If you live on the street, someone handing you money would be the least of your embarrassments. I was so ashamed of my own reactions.

Direction

I get asked for directions in New York all the time. The city is full of tourists. Lost tourists. Tourists who can't find a street or a store or a restaurant. Every day two or three ask me for directions. I feel sorry for them. They've asked the wrong person.

I have no sense of direction. I've sent people in all directions. I've sent them walking away from their destinations. I've sent them to the other side of Manhattan. Unintentionally.

At least I'm consistent in my misdirections. I usually point people to exactly where they don't want to go. 'Why don't you tell them to go in whatever direction you think it isn't?' my younger daughter said to me. She had just redirected a Chinese couple I had tried to be helpful to. 'They would have ended up back in China if they'd followed your directions,' my daughter said, after the couple had walked off.

I just sighed. I wasn't offended. I've adjusted to my

inadequate radar system. I've accepted the fact that I can't get my bearings with any degree of accuracy.

For a couple of years, I kept a compass in my purse. But I never trusted it. It was too fragile a gadget, I felt, to be really trustworthy. What a person like me needs is an instrument panel. Or a tracking station.

I can get lost anywhere. I get lost in hotels. I can't find my room easily. The arrows and room numbers on the hallway walls take me some time to take in. I've been known to get lost between my room and the lobby.

I failed to find the bathroom in my hotel room once. It was in the Savoy Hotel, in Berlin. The bathroom door was disguised as a large mirror. When the porter pointed this out to me, I felt stupid.

Everyone who knows me well gives me directions. Slowly and pointedly. I try not to take this as a sign of my lesser intelligence.

One of my most humiliating navigational errors occurred this year, in Vienna. A television crew was filming me. I had to walk towards the main door of St Stephan's Cathedral.

St Stephan's Cathedral is a large, flamboyant Romanesque and Gothic cathedral. It has a 137-metre-high Gothic bell tower, which is flanked by two 64-metre towers. It is in Stephansplatz, in the heart of Vienna.

The cameraman would be behind me, filming, the producer explained to me. The producer and I rehearsed the walk together. It took two minutes.

'Okay, start walking,' the soundman said to me. I set off. I walked at a moderate speed, so the crew could film the beautiful surroundings. I tried to look thoughtful, although I wasn't sure a thoughtful demeanour would be evident from a back view.

I walked some more and thought that St Stephan's should appear any second. But it didn't. I panicked. Where was the cathedral? I couldn't believe I could lose a large church.

But I had. I couldn't see St Stephan's anywhere. In the end, I had to turn back. The cameraman, the soundman and the producer were behind me, looking bewildered.

'What happened?' the producer asked me.

'I couldn't find the cathedral,' I answered. All three of them stared at me. 'I couldn't find it,' I repeated. The producer started laughing.

She walked me to the cathedral. It was to my left. I'd been looking straight ahead, and hadn't thought to turn my head.

'You can see that cathedral from Budapest,' my husband said when I told him I had missed it.

I saw the producer the next day, at a brunch in my honour. She was doubled up with laughter, in a corner of the room. 'She couldn't find it,' I could hear her saying. I started laughing myself.

Distance

I feel bad about living so far away from my father. It takes almost thirty hours to fly from New York to Australia, where he lives. You can't go there on a whim, or make an impromptu visit.

I miss him. And I miss seeing him. Each time we meet, I scan his face and his walk and his stance for signs of ageing. I worry that he is lonely in Australia. He is eighty-four. Most of his friends are dead.

I try not to call him when it is early in the morning, for him. He sometimes takes a sleeping pill, and if I catch him in that semi-conscious, not quite compos-mentis state, it can frighten me.

He's always been so bright. And I dread him losing any of that brightness. He dreads it himself. If I saw him, regularly, his half-asleep state wouldn't unnerve me.

Occasionally, I make wild plans for him to move to New York. A move that would be so expensive. And fraught with other complications.

Many people share my problem. It is a much more mobile world now. Many of us live a long way from our parents or our children.

In New York, elderly parents are sometimes seen as a storage problem. Where to place an elderly parent is a hot topic. A much-discussed question planned and plotted for with precision by middle-aged lawyers and bankers and other sons and daughters. What to do with your parents is a subject dreaded by an entire generation.

It is probably more difficult for New Yorkers to deal with elderly parents. People in New York are often older when they become parents. They can have to parent their children and their parents simultaneously. And they have parents who are too old to be used as babysitters.

Developers here foresaw this problem. There are now apartment buildings, on the Upper East Side, where you can park your parents and never have to worry about them. These apartments for the elderly have twenty-four hour supervision, access to medical treatment and highly organised social activities.

Your parents are kept as occupied as any nursery school child. Like the best preschools and kindergartens, enrolment is expensive.

For most people the cost of this storage is prohibitive. Which is possibly lucky for many parents. Or possibly not. Maybe these high-rise centres for later life make wonderful living arrangements.

In some ways, distance can be beneficial. My father and I don't experience the irritations or bad moods or disagreements that are present in everyone's existence. Our phone calls and visits are always special. The distance brings out the best in us.

This advantage doesn't make up for the disadvantages.

The comfort of being close by. The daily things you have to miss out on. It's not easy.

I periodically feel terrible for not having my father live with us. If he lived with us, it would make the move to New York more economically viable.

If he did move here, if he did move in with us, that wouldn't be easy either. That would be too close. For me. The lesser elements of both of us would be much more likely to emerge if we shared the same dwelling.

I sometimes think that the cost, the healthcare problems and the visa complexities of life here are convenient obstacles for me. I love my father. I love him dearly. But if he lived with me, he would drive me crazy. And I'd do the same to him.

I work at home. It would be impossible for me to concentrate with my father in the apartment.

'Would Grandpa really disturb you?' my younger daughter, who'd love her grandfather to live in New York, asked me.

'He'd drive me nuts, very quickly,' I said.

I paused. 'I don't want to ever hear you talking like that about me,' I said to her.

'You won't,' she said, 'I'll say it out of your hearing.'

Big City

L ife in a big city requires the oddest balancing act. Many people have a finely calibrated system of weights and measures in place in order to exist in a place like this.

They vacation regularly, go away for weekends, book evenings with friends. They exercise, meditate or join a yoga class. They seek psychic advice or employ someone to massage their physical being or their aura.

It's such a juggling act to stay afloat in an urban jungle. To stay human. To stay sane. To stay humane.

In New York, there is a new addition to the list of what you need to survive in the city. A new ingredient to make big city living more tolerable.

Dogs. Yes, dogs. The *New York Times* reported that quite a few companies have been encouraging their employees to bring their dogs to work.

The idea has been successful. People have been bringing poodles and dachshunds and terriers and German shepherds to the office. Now, an organisation, Pet Sitters International, has sponsored the first national observance of Take Your Dog To Work Day.

The *New York Times* said that people were more than willing to sacrifice their coffee breaks in order to take their dog outside for their toilet needs.

Dogs in the office helped to relieve stress, person after person said. A psychologist who specialises in the loss of a pet said a dog was the perfect pet to take to work. A cat, he said, would be too unnerved by a strange environment, whereas a dog would provide a 'pleasant exchange during the day'.

One New Yorker was quoted as saying that when he was off work ill for a month, his four-year-old bichon frisee still went to the office every day. A colleague picked up and returned the dog daily. The dog's owner explained that the dog couldn't stand staying at home all day.

A New York marketing firm has even sponsored contests for office dogs, with categories like Best Dressed and Most Obedient dog. Dogs added to the camaraderie of the office, the owner of the marketing company said.

What does this new trend mean? What does it say about us? Are our office environments and our lives so detached that we need a dog to make us feel more human? Is it so hard for us to interact with other humans? Is New York so anonymous that dogs make us feel more comfortable? Do we live with so much stress and tension that our dogs have to relax us?

It seems so. It seems to be a peculiarly New York phenomenon.

In New York companionship and comfort can come in the oddest forms. In a city that is hypersophisticated and chic, doing something unremarkably ordinary can be exhilarating.

Recently, I was sitting in my dentist's waiting room, on the eighteenth floor of the Rockefeller Center. I didn't want to be there. I've never liked dentists. But, here in America, I've encountered an additional problem. Flossing.

Americans are obsessed with flossing their teeth. Before I moved here, no one ever suggested I floss. Americans seem to floss day and night. I don't seem able to.

It's just about more than I can manage to communicate with my children, enjoy my husband, have a good relationship with my father and pacify my publishers. I can't fit in flossing.

So, I sat in the waiting room thinking up excuses for my failure to floss.

'Isn't the weather dismal?' a woman waiting for dental X-rays said to me. It was a very cold, very grey day.

We talked for ten minutes about how the weather in New York is never good. How it is either too cold, too windy, too wet, too hot or too humid.

The conversation was so intense, we could have been talking about our lovers or our mothers. We were in such accord. Such agreement. It was so satisfying. Such a pleasure.

Maybe instead of taking our dogs to work we should all congregate in dentists' waiting rooms.

Radishes

My German publisher is in town. She is looking for pumpkin seeds for her mother. Her mother wants to grow pumpkins, in Austria, where she lives. America apparently produces the best pumpkin seeds.

I offer to buy the seeds. There are two gardening stores close to where I live. I go to Grass Roots in Spring Street. The store is full of greenery. Palms, fronds, ferns and other plants. The air in the store is damp, good for the plants, I guess. Damp air is bad for my hair. It turns my curly hair into frizz. I have to leave.

I try Smith & Hawken on West Broadway. The air is nice and dry. I look around. You can buy, among other things, shears, sprinklers, soil scoops, hand rakes, hand weeders and mango pickers. I like them all. But then I like utensils and equipment. Kitchen equipment, medical, dental, architectural or engineering equipment.

I notice that everyone in the store looks peaceful, fulfilled. The customers and the staff. I want to be like that, too. I want to be one of them. I decide I will become a gardener. I will grow some radishes. I love radishes. I can say radish in several languages.

I buy a packet of Cherry Bomb radish seeds. These radishes will be lipstick-red, the packet says, and look especially attractive on plates of crudités or arranged like buds in a bowl of crushed ice.

I buy a large pot and some potting soil which has crushed oyster shells, peat moss, pumice, bat guano and earthworm castings. I buy plant food which contains magnesium, boron, copper, iron and zinc. And some liquid seaweed harvested off the 12,500-mile Norwegian coastline. Harvested at exactly where mineral-rich mountain waters, the Gulf Stream and arctic waters come together to produce perfect conditions for seaweed.

I go home and worry about where to place the pot. I choose a spot at the end of my fire escape. I check to make sure the radishes won't impede anyone's exit.

I plant them according to the directions. I feed them. It feels good. Reminiscent of being pregnant and swallowing vitamin C and folic acid. The radishes will be ready for picking twenty-five days after planting, the packet tells me. The seedlings should emerge in seven to ten days.

I feel pleased with myself. I've done everything right. This is the right season. Late spring. The nights are still cool enough for ideal radish-growing conditions. I look forward to seeing my seedlings.

I check my radishes every day. I feel close to the soil. At one with nature. This is what farmers must feel like. I plan a series of radish meals.

On day ten, there are still no seedlings. I pace around the fire escape. Then I walk to the Union Square market and question a vegetable seller about radish seedlings. 'They should come up any day,' she says. They don't.

I complain to my younger daughter. 'It's not Jewish to be able to grow vegetables, anyway,' I say when I've finished complaining.

'I've grown tomatoes and basil and my own carrots,' she says.

'Yes, but you've got a non-Jewish father,' I tell her.

Maybe I overfed the radishes? I have a tendency to overfeed people. After twenty-four days, a few leaves appear. I'm not that excited at their appearance. I'm a bit disheartened.

A week later, I decide that it is time for picking. I pull up my radishes. A reedy little runt of a radish appears. I go to Gourmet Garage, in Broome Street, and buy two bunches of radishes.

And, yes. I did buy the pumpkin seeds. I bought eight varieties. They are now probably halfway through growing into hundreds of pumpkins.

Religion

I wish I had God in my life. I wish I had religion. These are new wishes. They arrived relatively recently.

I've never been religious. Never had a religion.

I am Jewish. I am Jewish by birth. Bound to my Jewishness by tradition, by culture and by history. Not by religious teaching.

Religion was as forbidden to me as a teenager as sex.

I grew up with parents who preached God's absence. There is no God, they said, over and over again. For them God's absence was palpable. When they were lost in Auschwitz and the Lodz Ghetto for six years, and lost everyone they loved, no God was evident.

They had both come from religious homes before they were rounded up and imprisoned. After it was over, it was impossible for either of them to be a believer.

I wasn't allowed to go to synagogue. My parents felt dismissive of those who thought there was a God. I felt disloyal if I even looked at a synagogue. There was one in our street, and I used to stride by it quickly.

Today, when I experience a longing or an inclination or a need to encompass religion, I still feel that disloyalty. It is very confusing.

Religion seems to smooth out uncertainty. Life, by its very nature, I know, has to be uncertain. But I hate uncertainties. I want to nail everything down. Make it certain. With religion, uncertainties seem less uncertain. I can see the attraction in that.

And in the structure and order that religion imposes. I've always loved structure and routine and order. Whether it is present in work or in exercise or in the confines of a diet.

Many people are reassured by structure and order. Look at the difficulties and problems men face on retirement.

The order and routine of being a writer suits me. I am a very orderly writer. I make neat notes. I colour code and number them. I line my pens and other accoutrements up in tidy and precise rows.

The routines of religion have mesmerised me for years. I have watched Catholics handling rosary beads until I am almost hypnotised. I have felt the same magnetic attraction to Jews tying their phylacteries, or Moslems kneeling and bending in prayer to Allah.

It reassures me that there is more to life than the moment before us.

Another reassuring aspect of religion is its link with the past. A past that seems more lasting than the memory of last week's vacation or last year's school reunion.

Religion also provides a sense of belonging. Which seems more essential in this more mobile, less intimate universe. And a sense of community. Many of our communities are now comprised of work colleagues and transient visitors. Especially those of us who live in big cities. We live among strangers and acquaintances.

In New York, where I have lived for ten years, I have no one who knew my mother. And few people who know my father. Two of my three children live here. Many people I know have never met them.

I have no old friends in the city. No people I can be on less than my best behaviour with. For me there is no continuity, no link with the past. Everything can seem fleeting. Temporary.

No wonder religion looks tempting.

I used to look at religious figures, rabbis and priests, with awe. I used to think they had answers to unanswerable dilemmas and questions. But I've met rabbis and priests who complained and argued and felt as aggrieved over petty annoyances as anyone else.

I've met rabbis and priests who seem as confused and self-righteous and prejudiced as most of us. I've met few rabbis or priests who seemed wiser and more resolved than the average person. The average priest or rabbi seems as average as the rest of us.

Sex

Sex isn't usually something I discuss with friends. Occasionally we talk about sex in abstract terms. But we don't discuss each other's sex lives. Recently, this changed.

Three female friends, all in their mid-thirties and married, separately, and almost matter-of-factly, brought up the subject of sex. Each time, I was bothered by what was said. And surprised at my own reluctance to pursue the matter further.

'I've got no time for sex,' one of the friends said to me. I had asked her if managing her job was more stressful now that she had a baby. 'I can manage the job and the baby,' she said. 'But I've got no time for sex.' I blushed as though I was a teenager. And felt tongue-tied.

'I hope I don't miscarry,' said a newly pregnant friend, 'I'd have to have sex again.' Her voice and expression suggested that it had been more than difficult, possibly even tedious, to orchestrate the current pregnancy. I didn't ask why.

The third friend told me she was trying to get pregnant. 'We're going away for the weekend,' she said, 'I'll be ovulating.' An ovulation assignation, I thought. It sounded quite exciting. 'I've written it into his diary and mine,' she said. 'Sex on Saturday and sex on Sunday.' It still didn't sound too bad. 'It's particularly good timing,' she said. 'It's so much more difficult to orchestrate sex during the week.'

I was quiet. New Yorkers have busy lives. Everyone knows that. New Yorkers have no time. I didn't know this included no time for sex. I know that many aspects of sex are difficult. I sometimes write about sex. In novels. This has caused me several edgy moments as a mother. 'I just skip the yucky bits,' my younger daughter said to me, while reading one of my novels, when she was thirteen.

For another novel I needed to know how much sperm the average male ejaculated. I asked my son. He was a medical student at the time. He raised his eyebrows at me. I think he would have preferred a question about a different subject.

Sex drives people crazy in unexpected ways. I think that half of the frenzied hostility directed at President Clinton during the Lewinsky scandal was propelled by resentment and jealousy of his libido.

Male politician after male politician was grim lipped and stern jawed as they referred heatedly to Clinton's criminality. I thought it was possibly Clinton's sexuality that was making them froth at the mouth. I noticed that it was the more joyless and juiceless of politicians who displayed the most disgust.

Sex can be upsetting. A parrot in a hotel I stayed in, in a small town in Mexico, startled the guests at breakfast each morning with his feverish grunts, groans and sighs. His low-pitched grunts were interspersed with higher, more tremulous sighs. And breathlessness.

I knew the parrot was new to the hotel. 'Whoever owned him had a lot of sex,' I said to my husband. The parrot was a big success with the Mexican guests. It made them laugh. The Americans were not quite as enthusiastic. Some of them looked strained.

I found the bird disconcerting. He screamed and whispered and panted and growled with such abandon. I began to feel embarrassed and awkward. And, finally, intimidated. The parrot was making me feel inadequate. 'I don't growl like that,' I said to my husband. 'I'm not even sure I moan.'

'Who owned this parrot?' I asked one of the waiters.

'A couple,' he replied.

'A young couple?' I said.

'No,' he said. 'They were an old couple.'

'How old?' I said.

'Middle aged,' he said.

I decided the conversation was veering in a dangerous direction. I didn't want to discuss what stage of middle age was old enough to be old. I already felt elderly.

Shorts

One of the things that makes the end of summer and the approach of winter more bearable is the thought of not seeing any more Americans in shorts.

Americans are obsessed with shorts. As soon as the temperature rises above 65 degrees Fahrenheit, Americans bring out their shorts. In large numbers.

All sorts of shorts appear, with humans inside them. Shorts with zebras printed on them, shorts with checks and tartans. Khaki shorts, fluorescent shorts.

Shorts with flowers all over them are the worst sort. And could put you off gardening for life.

Americans love shorts. They love walking around with their legs showing. Which is understandable if you happen to be the owner of Madonna, Michael Jordan or Raquel Welch's legs. Which most Americans are not.

They seem to overlook this, though, in the national obsession to put their legs into shorts. One day of hot weather, and the whole country is in shorts. Small shorts, long shorts, large shorts, short shorts. Everybody is sporting shorts.

Some of them shouldn't be. On a very hot day the sight of a thin pair of pale hairy legs protruding from bright red shorts doesn't do anything for me. Some things are best covered up. There are some things the rest of us shouldn't be subjected to.

But the question of whether you should be wearing shorts or not is not a question Americans ask themselves. Like freedom of speech, Americans believe the ability to wear shorts is a basic human right.

In a city as chic and sophisticated as New York you'd think you'd see fewer shorts. But you don't. People who for the rest of the year look glamorous and self-assured, in summer suddenly turn up looking as though they're about to attend a relative's barbecue.

A chic black dress or a Hugo Boss suit can cover up a lot. Shorts can't. This can prove to be beneficial to you. Shorts take away some of the mystique that can make you nervous or in awe of someone.

In a city in which it is easy to feel awkward and inconsequential in the presence of people more powerful than you, having that person in shorts can be a good equaliser. It is much harder to feel intimidated by a shorts wearer.

Most people don't look their best in shorts. Shorts reveal more of our flaws and blemishes than most other items of clothing.

I've never worn shorts. For very good reason. I look terrible in them. I'd lose any credibility I have and all of my dignity if I were to wear shorts.

I think you've got to have great legs, or at least good ones, to wear shorts. And I haven't. So I don't wear them, even though I'm trying hard to fit in here. Trying to be more American. I've tried to tone down my Australian vowels, and, after ten years, I've learnt to speak more speedily.

Trying to be American can be exhausting. I've practised perkiness until I'm blue in the face. And still perkiness eludes me. It's not my natural condition.

Nor is friendliness. I'm just not a naturally friendly person. I'm reserved with strangers and people I don't know well. One look at my subdued demeanour and Americans know I'm not one of them.

But there's hope for me yet. I have caught on to an American passion. I've become addicted to basketball. I don't play it, I watch it. I've become a devoted follower of the New York Knicks. I watch all the Knicks' games on television. I can't bear it when the team loses. And my blood pressure soars when the game is close.

This year the Knicks made it to the National Basketball League's finals. They lost the cup final, by one point. I was depressed for days. And felt truly American.

I liked the feeling. I branched out and tried pancakes and maple syrup for breakfast. It wasn't too bad an experience.

But no matter how it might help me fit in, I draw the line at some things. I will never wear shorts.

Christmas

I n New York at Christmas, it's business as usual. This holiday, which in many parts of the world causes things to come to a stop, doesn't derail New York.

I like the fact that stores stay open, that cafes still welcome you. I don't like it when cities shut down, when everything closes. It always makes me feel desolate, and on my own, when the streets of a city are deserted and you can't buy fresh bread or fresh milk.

This is irrational of me. I never drink milk and I try to be moderate about the amount of bread I eat.

For some reason, though, I need to know that everything is open. I like the busyness of cities. I like the feeling that everything is functioning. That everything is up and running.

When the postman is delivering mail and the store-keepers are selling their wares I feel happy. I feel part of all of the activity. Without it, I feel curiously empty.

The fact that I am not a Christian, that I am Jewish,

is, of course, part of the reason I feel excluded at Christmas. I'd clearly feel less lonely, less left out, if I were busy celebrating the traditions and rituals. But it is not the whole explanation.

Other public holidays, like New Year's Eve, affect me in the same way. I don't like seeing the world silent. For whatever reason, normal everyday activities reassure me. New York is never quiet. Not even at Christmas.

Christmas greetings can be a political minefield in this city. And New Yorkers know this. They don't assume that everyone is a Christian. Merry Christmas is not what New Yorkers automatically say to each other.

The non-denominational phrase, 'Happy Holidays', is in heavy use in New York in the Christmas season. And that is how it should be, in a city heavily populated with Buddhists, Hindus, Sikhs, Moslems, Jews and non-Christian African Americans.

In Australia, where I grew up, everyone said Merry Christmas to everyone else. Jewish people said Merry Christmas to Chinese people. Some Jews wished each other a Happy Christmas. Everyone felt the need to blend in.

In Australia, the whole country seemed to close for Christmas, which of course, in that part of the world, occurs in mid-summer, in often blisteringly hot weather.

To counter the effect of the celebration occurring in the wrong season, Australians spray their windows and their Christmas trees with a white substance that comes out of a can. It is sticky and is supposed to simulate snow.

When I was a child, the suburbs were filled with white-sprayed houses. Rotund Father Christmases stood on street corners, in city centres, ringing bells, or walked through department stores handing out gifts.

They were dressed in thick, padded, red and white costumes and gloves, hats and boots. They were supposed to be spreading cheer and goodwill. Most of them looked stressed and hot. In danger of collapsing with heat exhaustion.

Christmas Day in Australia is altogether an overheated occasion. People are in their houses roasting and baking turkeys, chickens and hams. They are standing in hot kitchens stirring sauces and steaming plum puddings, in sweltering heat.

The food is eaten in the middle of the day. It is not nouvelle cuisine. Digesting this festive fare in temperatures that can reach a hundred degrees is no mean feat. At the end of the Christmas Day meal, many Australians can do little more than desperately search for an Alka-Seltzer.

As a child, I loved Christmas Day. When the weather became too hot to bear, my parents would take me to the beach. They both worked in factories and always got Christmas off.

We would go to the beach in the late afternoon and stay until late evening. My mother would pack a picnic of cucumber salad, sliced beets, lettuce, cold boiled eggs, schnitzels and watermelon.

If I was lucky, an ice-cream vendor would come by, and I would be allowed to have a chocolate-coated ice cream on a stick. It was the best part of Christmas.

New Year's Eve

I started worrying about what to do on New Year's Eve, the last night of the twentieth century, months beforehand.

I felt I should do something special. The thought of doing something ordinary, like going to bed early as I have done on many a New Year's Eve, made me feel as though I'd be missing out. Although I wasn't sure what it was I'd be missing out on.

I started asking people what they were doing on New Year's Eve. I asked friends and acquaintances. Some people had firm plans – a yacht on the Florida Keys, a house in Rio de Janeiro, a trek through the Himalayas. Others hadn't decided. No one asked me to join them.

I asked some more people what they were doing. I tried not to look plaintive. I tried not to look as though I was angling for an invitation. I didn't want to appear friendless, or socially undesirable. Everyone discussed their plans, or lack of plans, wholeheartedly. But none of them invited me anywhere.

I began to feel depressed. 'We haven't been besieged by invitations to celebrate the end of the millennium,' I said to my husband.

'So what?' he said. 'You don't like New Year's Eve anyway,' he added.

He's right. I don't like New Year's Eve. I don't like the thought of big endings. Or big beginnings. They make me nervous. Make me feel I should dredge up grand thoughts and proposals and resolutions instead of the usual flotilla of small understandings and undertakings.

As well, most of the New Year's Eve festivities I've been to have seemed forced. I've felt forced myself. Forced to look as though I'm having a good time.

But this New Year's Eve felt different. More momentous than the normal progression of one year to the next. I felt I should witness the changing of the centuries.

Intellectually, I knew there'd be nothing to see, but I couldn't shake off the feeling that I should be present.

We'd go somewhere, I decided. I didn't want to stay in New York. New York is as unruly an environment as I can tolerate on normal days. I suspected it would be mayhem at the end of the millennium.

Maybe we'd go to Mexico, I thought. I love Mexico. Or maybe Las Vegas. I've always wanted to go to Las Vegas. We could see the Siegfried and Roy show in Las Vegas.

Siegfried Fischbacher and Roy Uwe Ludwig Horn, Siegfried and Roy, are the most successful entertainers in the history of Las Vegas. On stage the two flamboyantly costumed and coiffed illusionists, I had read, make twenty-four tigers, eight lions, an Arabian horse and an elephant, as well as themselves, vanish and reappear.

There is something mesmerising about Siegfried and Roy's perfectly chiselled cheekbones, chunky gold jewellery, startling suntans and shirts open to the waist. I think they must awaken the more gaudy, flashy parts of me. Parts that are mostly dormant.

Forty years ago, Siegfried and Roy were poor young immigrants from Germany. Now, over seven hundred thousand people a year come to Las Vegas to see them. I wanted to see them, too, I decided.

I spent two days talking to travel agents. Talking about plane reservations and possible Y2K problems. In the end I couldn't bring myself to make a booking. The thought of being stranded in Las Vegas because of a Y2K glitch had dampened my enthusiasm.

I resigned myself to staying at home. At least at home I'd have the bottled water I'd been stockpiling and the cans of sardines and salmon and tuna and baked beans I'd been accumulating. And the can openers and batteries and torches.

I bought all of this despite President Clinton's announcement that America was prepared for the new millennium. There would be no computer mishaps, he said. No Y2K problems.

As everyone now knows, the transition into the next century was very smooth. I, however, am still eating cans of sardines and salmon and baked beans.

Sport

An Australian newspaper asked me to write an article on sport. It was for an issue devoted to the Sydney 2000 Olympics.

I laughed when the editor commissioned the piece. Sport has always tripped me up, I said to the editor. And it has.

Some of my worst childhood memories are to do with sport. I still cringe when I remember how, at thirteen, I would try to hoist myself over the vaulting horse while a group of boys hung out of their classroom window, howling with laughter.

Several of them always seemed to be in the vicinity when my gymnastics class was in progress. They used to double up with mirth at the sight of me trying to somersault on the balance beam. I had no chance. I couldn't somersault on flat ground, let alone elevated on a thin bench.

One of the boys reported me to the gymnastics

teacher for spinning my run around the school oval out long enough to finish at the same time as those who'd done six laps.

No one in my family, as far as I know, has ever been athletic. We had few living relatives, but neither my mother nor father ever mentioned a family member's prowess at sport when they talked about the past.

Athleticism doesn't seem to be something we Bretts were blessed with. My father drives his car half a block to pick up a carton of milk. He's good at parking. Not walking.

That's not quite true any longer. He's been walking for forty minutes a day, as a favour to me. I want him to be healthy and live to one hundred. He's eighty-four.

Every few days, he calls me from Australia to complain about the walking. I tell him to keep doing it. 'You'll learn to enjoy it,' I said recently.

'That's what you said two years ago,' he said, 'I still don't like it.'

'I'm sure it's doing you good,' I said.

'I'm not so sure,' he said.

I discovered walking when I was forty. Before that, I was my father's daughter. A good parker.

I began my walking career by walking at a normal pace. I then sped up until I metamorphosed into a power walker. And a walking addict.

I walk every day and I treadmill. I could almost, albeit belatedly, be considered athletic. I love my treadmill. Some days I don't want to get off it.

Last summer I was treadmilling uphill for an hour and forty minutes every morning. I think I was making up for lost time and trying to erase the image of the failed somersaulter.

I've cut down now to an hour and ten minutes, which some people feel is still excessive. 'Why do you have to do things to such extremes?' asked my younger daughter.

'Too much moderation is not good for you,' I said. She looked disapproving.

'You walk too much,' my father said to me last week when I said I was feeling tired.

'Exercise gives you more energy, makes you less tired,' I said.

'You are crazy,' he replied.

Which is exactly what my daughter said when I said I didn't want to learn the charleston or the lindy hop or the jitterbug. This younger daughter loves dancing. Swing dancing is her latest passion.

In New York, you can swing dance any night of the week. Swing dancing has experienced a big revival. Thousands of New Yorkers are dancing the hop rock and the boogie-woogie. I won't be joining them.

I'm full of admiration for people who kick up their heels when they hear music. When the music starts, I become grounded. A paralysis sets in. The tempo of whatever is playing eludes me. When I hear music, I don't move my hips or click my fingers. I freeze.

I can't even clap to a beat. My claps are always out of sync with everyone else's. I have rhythm in my soul, but not in my limbs. I'm better off sticking to my treadmill.

Busy

In New York your status would slip, instantly, if you were to admit to having time to spare. If you were to admit to being unoccupied, to being idle, for even a brief period of time, your desirability would dip, violently.

It would be social and professional suicide to ever let anyone know that you were doing nothing.

In this city, people's ratings plummet if they confess to being anything less than frantic. In New York it is essential to appear busy. Being busy is more than a status symbol. It is a necessity, a prerequisite for being a New Yorker.

Looking relaxed will disadvantage you, will make people suspicious. A carefree demeanour is a stigma, not an asset, in Manhattan. In a city that measures success in terms of filling every available moment with some form of stress, having time on your hands suggests that you are not successful.

Having no time for leisure, no time for family, no

time for friends, is a position New Yorkers aspire to. It is a prestigious state, admired and endorsed by all who live here.

Everyone loves to tell you how busy they are. From CEOs to the unemployed. They are all perpetually occupied and constantly in a rush. They are on a committee or taking a class, or arranging a meeting, or else they have ten things pending.

'My day is crazy', is something you often hear stated. It doesn't mean that what the speaker is doing is crazy, it means they are busy. 'My day/week/month/year/life is crazy', is a common expression.

It would be the kiss of death to say you were bored or restless. Or at a loss for what to do next. Looking unoccupied will make you an outcast, even if you are young, rich and beautiful. Being busy is what counts. Above all else.

The Mayor of New York, Rudolph Guiliani, sets a good example for New Yorkers to follow. He takes pride in the fact that he never takes vacations.

He is a workaholic. He makes pronouncements and announcements. He offers explanations and justifications. And congratulations and condolences. He is on television every night and in the newspapers every day.

He is always working. And in a rush. He lost a lot of weight when he first took office. Maybe he was too rushed to eat? Guiliani isn't the only one in a hurry. All New Yorkers are in a rush.

There is a lot of activity in this hyperactive city. New Yorkers faced with free time race to fill it up. A gap in a schedule is merely something to be plugged with classes or lessons or exercise sessions.

And a vacation has to be planned with precision, and

has to be perfect. The accommodation, the location, the climate and the other guests have to be just right. There is no time to waste.

New Yorkers don't like to pause. This is not a reflective city. Everyone is too busy. There is a New York 'I'm so busy' monologue. It lasts for ten minutes. I know. I've delivered it myself.

What has happened to time? What has happened to time to spare? To long days and long nights? Everything is short and swift now. Everything has sped up.

We have no time. No time for our parents. No time for our children. No time for ourselves. What has happened to us? Why are we all so busy? Is there so much to do? Is there more than there used to be?

I don't remember my parents being perpetually busy. They seemed to have time. Time to entertain, time to go to the movies, time to go dancing.

I'm so tired at the end of the day, that even if I was more than the mediocre dancer that I am, even if I was Ginger Rogers, I don't think I would go dancing.

Knitting

A woman I saw, briefly, on a bus a few days ago, created havoc in my life.

I was on the M8 bus, which travels across town and back, on Eighth Street. She was sitting two seats away from me, and she was knitting.

I couldn't take my eyes off her knitting. She was using green metallic knitting needles and maroon wool. I could hear the small, steady click of the knitting needles as they went in and out of the stitches.

A desperate urge to knit came over me. I wanted to ask her if I could knit a row. But it's hard enough to talk to a stranger on a bus in New York about something innocuous, let alone ask them if you can handle their knitting.

So, I said nothing. I just sat there lusting after her knitting.

By the time I got off the bus, I was enveloped by an overwhelming need to knit.

I haven't knitted for years. For decades. I'm not even a good knitter. I'm at my best when there are no curves in the garment I'm attempting to knit. This limits me to scarves and square sweaters.

I was bothered by this need the woman in the bus had unleashed in me. Agitated, really. Who needs to knit? Not me, I told myself. I tried to banish all knitting thoughts from my head. But it didn't work. My need to knit grew. I gave up. I decided I'd have to give in to this knitting fixation. I'd have to buy some knitting wool and some knitting needles.

But where? New York is not a city one immediately associates with knitting. I couldn't think of one place that might sell knitting wool or needles. And I couldn't think of anyone I knew who would know, either.

Anyway, it wasn't a question I wanted to put to friends. A need to knit is not necessarily something you want to broadcast about yourself.

I got out the New York telephone directory. I found Knit Knot, Knit Tech, Knitomania, Knitown. I called them all.

'What?' said one person after another.

'Knitting wool,' I said.

'What?' they repeated. You'd have thought I was speaking Latin or Etruscan.

'I want to buy knitting wool,' I shouted into the phone. 'I want to buy wool to knit with.' None of them stocked it.

I wasn't daunted. Woolworths, I thought. Surely Woolworths would sell wool. Then I remembered, there was no longer a Woolworths in Manhattan. The last one closed over two years ago.

But there was a Kmart. A huge Kmart on Astor Place.

You can buy camping equipment, pharmaceutical goods, car jacks and bras in Kmart. They'd be bound to sell knitting wool.

'No,' said the Kmart telephonist.

'Do you know where I could buy some?' I said.

'Maybe Fourteenth Street,' she said.

I decided to go straight there. I couldn't concentrate on anything else anyway.

I walked slowly along Fourteenth Street, from Avenue A until Tenth Avenue, a long walk. There was no knitting wool shop. I felt dispirited.

I was on Sixth Avenue on my way home, when the unexpected occurred. I looked up and saw a sign above a store. Knitting wool, it said.

Upstairs was a world of knitting. Knitting patterns, wools, needles, stitch holders and stitch counters. I looked for metallic green knitting needles. They didn't have them. I bought enormous plastic ones instead. And very thick wool to go with the very thick needles. This would be time saving. Thick wool knits up very quickly. I bought a row counter too, because I'd never had one.

I decided to knit a rectangular hat. I began in bed that night. I cast on what looked like the right number of stitches. And started. But it didn't feel quite right. The huge needles were unwieldy. I kept denting my husband's elbow with my left needle. I knitted four rows. It wasn't at all satisfying.

Three rows later I gave up. If anyone wants a quarter of a rectangular hat, it is in my cupboard.

The Cat

My younger daughter, who lives in the East Village, has adopted a cat. She had to guarantee, in writing, among other things, that she would not declaw the cat, and she would not allow him to go outside – too many germs.

My daughter adopted this cat from a woman who, once a week, stands near the corner of Broadway and Prince Street, with several stray cats she hopes to find homes for.

I hadn't wanted my daughter to get a cat. 'New York is not a place for pets,' I said to her.

'New York,' she said, 'is exactly the sort of place you need a pet in. You work so hard you have no social life. At least I'll have a cat to come home to.'

She got the cat. He already had a name. Lancelot. She started pestering me to come and meet Lancelot. 'He's a very handsome cat,' she said. I gave in and went to her apartment for a formal introduction to the cat.

Lancelot did indeed turn out to be a very handsome cat. With fur that has an aesthetically appealing reddish tinge. When my daughter picked him up, he put his paws around her neck and purred. I was impressed.

Two days after my visit with Lancelot, I was walking up Sixth Avenue. My daughter had called me that morning to report on Lancelot's progress. So far no problems, she said.

The woman who had adopted Lancelot out had suggested that if my daughter encountered any problems with the cat, she should consult a pet communicator, someone who had been professionally trained to talk to cats. I didn't even begin to wonder what sort of professional training would qualify you to talk to cats.

On the corner of Waverley Place, a woman was dragging a reluctant child by the arm. 'You're driving me nuts,' she was saying to the child. I sympathised. I understand the feeling of imminent dementia that motherhood can bring on.

Two blocks later, a woman I passed was admonishing a six or seven year old. 'Do you want me to put you in an orphanage?' she said loudly to him. The kid appeared unmoved by the threat. I looked more worried than he did.

I walked on. On Ninth Street, outside Balducci's, one of the most heavenly food stores in the world, a woman was tying her dog to a post. 'Sweetie pie,' she said to the dog, 'I'm just going in for some asparagus and some strawberries. I'll only be five minutes and I'll be right back.' She waved to the dog as she repeated that she would be right back.

I didn't want to draw any rash conclusions about New Yorkers and their attitudes towards pets and children.

I thought about a scene I'd witnessed last year, a week before Christmas. Father Christmas was sitting in the window of Beasty Feasts, a pet-supplies store on Hudson Street in the West Village. On Father Christmas's lap was a large black dog. A pointed red and green hat was on the dog's head and a red scarf was wound around his neck.

Around Father Christmas was an array of photographic equipment and lights. And a photographer and a photographer's assistant. The photographer looked flustered. His assistant was in a sweat. They were trying to get the black dog to face the camera instead of the street. Eventually they got the shot.

Jasper and Jason, two golden retrievers, were next to be photographed. Together. At Father Christmas's feet. Jason sat and looked at the camera but not Jasper. 'Sit, Jasper, sit,' Jasper's owner shouted at him. But Jasper wanted to stand. 'Sit, Jasper, sit,' Father Christmas said sternly. Jasper wagged his tail and knocked over several pots of poinsettias and some carefully hung silver stars and bells. The store manager looked distraught.

I couldn't stop laughing. I laughed so much I was in pain. I left before the photographer managed to capture Jasper and Jason's visit to Father Christmas.

Walking home, I thought that maybe my daughter was right. Maybe New York is the perfect place to have a pet.

The Queue

I am standing in the queue for the women's toilets at a Broadway theatre. It is 7.45 p.m. The play begins at 8 p.m. It is a typical theatre-going queue. The women are aged between thirty and seventy. Everyone is self-contained and self-assured. No one speaks. This is New York. And in New York you still don't speak to strangers.

I look at my watch. I've already been waiting for five minutes. The queue has hardly moved.

The men's toilets are next door. Men are going in and men are coming out. Man after man emerges looking pleased, purposeful. 'You'd think someone would realise that they need to reduce the size of the men's toilets and expand the women's,' I say. A rumble of agreement goes through the queue.

'They've expanded the women's toilets at the Vivian Beaumont Theater at the Lincoln Center,' a woman at the back of the queue says. I make a mental note of this.

'We're going to miss the opening scene,' a woman says.

'I always get to the theatre fifteen minutes early,' says another woman, tersely.

'Me, too,' I say.

We all stand there, 'Excuse me,' a young woman says to me, 'where do you get your hair cut?' I tell her. 'Is it expensive?' she says. I nod, a bit shamefacedly. I wish that I was the sort who got cheap hair cuts.

'I pay $150 for my haircuts,' the woman standing next to me says. 'I pay $175 for my colour,' another woman says. Suddenly, we are exchanging the burdens and costs of maintaining the appearance of genetically blessed looks. Everyone in the queue is smiling. A cosiness, rare in New York, envelops us.

When we stop talking, we see that the queue has barely moved. We fall silent. Men continue to emerge from the men's toilet. They look happy. Nobody in our queue looks happy. Some of us look grim.

'Why don't we use the men's toilets?' an English woman says. There is a silence. A few of us shift around uncomfortably. 'We've all seen a penis before,' she says. There is more silence.

'I think the sight of so many strange penises might be overwhelming,' I say. I correct myself. 'I don't mean strange penises,' I say, 'I mean strangers' penises.' Some-one laughs.

'Let's just go in there,' the English woman says. No one moves. A pall has fallen over us. A shadow. A cloud. Women look at their feet.

'We're supposed to be tough New Yorkers,' a woman in her thirties says.

'I'll be very quick when it's my turn,' I whisper to the woman behind me.

'Well I'm going to the men's toilets,' the English woman says and strides inside. We all look at her as though she's gone to Mars or Jupiter. We look at each other.

'I can't do it,' I say.

'Neither can I,' the woman in front of me says.

'I don't want to,' a blonde woman says.

An elderly woman starts laughing. 'It's pathetic, isn't it?' I say. 'All these women afraid of a few penises.' I start laughing, too. Soon we are all laughing. I laugh so hard I have to wipe the tears from my eyes. The English woman reappears. Apparently unharmed.

A few minutes later, it is my turn to go to the toilet. I don't want to go. I don't want to leave the group. I feel like a four year old. I want to say, 'Can we be friends?'

But this is New York. And what do you do? Exchange business cards? I go to the toilet. I am quick. I come out. I want to say 'What's your name?' to a few of the women. But I don't. I wave goodbye and go to my seat. The play? It was very boring.

Unhealthy

I often shop at health-food stores. I'm largely vegetarian. I buy organically grown fruit and vegetables and grains. And feel that they are healthier than those products that aren't labelled organic.

You can buy products that contain no animal fats, no synthetic preservatives, no chemical additives, no engineered ingredients, no artificial colours or fragrances.

You can buy food grown without pesticides and fertilisers. You can buy food with no salt, no sugar, no caffeine, no saccharine. You can buy flaxseed or oats distributed through every conceivable concoction, and wheat-free and gluten-free organically grown bagels.

The choice is bewildering. As are some of the products. I recently spent ten minutes trying to work out what Born Again Pain Relief Crème could be.

Advice, which seems to be dispensed in abundance in most health-food stores, can also be bewildering. You can be the recipient of advice about irrigating your colon or refreshing your epiglottis.

'It's very unhealthy to drink cold water in the morning. It shocks your organs,' the cashier at a health-food store said to me. I'd stopped for a bottle of water, after an early morning walk.

I've been drinking cold water, in the morning, for years. Had I been shocking my organs, I wondered? Were they perpetually on edge? In a state of continual tension? Could this be the cause of my anxiety prone temperament?

I left the store, quickly. I didn't want to probe any further into my shocked organs.

Health-food stores are full of people meeting their daily essential fatty acid quotient. And people making sure that their provisions provide the requisite amount of anti-oxidants and electrolytes.

What bothers me, is that they don't look healthy. They are often pale and pinched. With lacklustre skin, lank hair and a damp demeanour. They look far less healthy than those who shop in supermarkets.

People who eat at McDonald's might be a bit chubby, but they seem robust and full of life next to health-food store customers.

In health-food stores, the clientele can also be self-righteous. Sure of their own decisions, their own beliefs.

I've been accosted by proselytisers of aloe vera and ginseng and horse-tail cuttings. I'd prefer to chat to a hamburger addict.

Health-food customers are sometimes unhinged. More unhinged, it seems to me, than the average hot-dog lover.

I was buying some farm-raised catfish at my local health-food shop, when I was approached by a fellow customer. 'You know farmed catfish are raised in the same way as factory farmed chickens,' she said to me. I nodded politely and turned away.

'They are no different from battery hens and cows in pens,' she said.

'I'm in a hurry,' I said to the man behind the counter who was weighing my fillets.

'The catfish's parents only exist as breeder fish,' the woman said. 'Their only purpose in life is to produce little catfish children for you to consume.'

I wished she'd go away. I love fish. As a meal, I mean. Not as a pet or a playmate. I tried to look unfriendly.

She tried another tack. 'You probably think this catfish is perfectly safe to eat,' she said. 'Fish farmers use disinfectants and herbicides and vaccines and medicines. Farmed fish can have the same chemical residues you find in cattle.'

I didn't know what to do. I looked to the man who was serving me. He was no help. He just went on wrapping my fillets.

'That's not all,' the woman said. 'Farmed fish can escape and mate with other fish in the area. This is bad for the gene pool. Makes for weaker offspring.

'The world's rivers and oceans are already depleted,' she added.

The shop assistant handed me my fillets. I grabbed my catfish and ran for the exit. I left the store looking wan and exhausted.

Tests

Because of the complex nature of health-care coverage in America, I've had seven or eight different family doctors in ten years.

This was due to the high turnover of doctors working for the health maintenance organisation I belonged to.

I found it stressful to be continually introducing myself to my new physician. To have to explain my physical and emotional quirks at each visit. To have to go through my medical history, again and again.

Reiterating my fairly uneventful medical history always causes me to feel unwell. I leave the doctor's rooms certain that a major illness is about to fell me.

Last year, I managed to change health-care companies. The new plan allowed me to more or less choose the family doctor I wanted. I chose a doctor around the corner. The local pharmacist had recommended him. I think the doctor I chose is quite good. But I'm not sure. I've hardly seen him.

On my first visit to his rooms, I was looked after by a medical student. I was there for an annual check-up.

This medical student was determined to leave no part of me unchecked. He was very thorough, very deliberate and very slow. By the time he was finished, I was a nervous wreck.

I had to do eye exercises and deep and shallow breathing, and intricate leg, knee and arm movements. I was tapped and thumped and prodded. He wrote copious notes after each of these procedures. My anxiety level rose with each word he wrote.

An hour later, the family doctor walked into the room. He looked through the medical student's voluminous notes. 'You've been very thorough,' he said to him. The student looked pleased, although I thought I detected some sarcasm in the doctor's voice.

The student began a ten-minute report on his findings. I felt almost sick with tension. Sure I was going to hear something unpleasant. 'The patient is female,' the student began. I felt myself sigh with relief. So far the information was not too difficult to handle.

It turned out that there was nothing wrong. I seemed to be in quite good shape, according to the student. I was about to get dressed and leave when the doctor suggested that I have a sigmoidoscopy, an examination of the colon and rectum, as well as my annual mammogram and Pap smear, and, because of a family history of ovarian cancer, an ultrasound of my ovaries.

I dread these sorts of tests. I operate on the illogical principle that problems you are ignorant of don't exist. But I went ahead and made the appointments.

The technician who performed the ultrasound sighed a few minutes into the procedure. 'Your bowel is in the way of one of your ovaries,' she said.

'Really?' I said. I was disturbed. Who needs to know stuff like this? Not me.

'Yes,' she said. 'It is moving.' I didn't know bowels shifted around. I panicked. Maybe they didn't? Maybe it was only my bowel that was restless?

'It's good that it moves,' she said. I relaxed. I decided not to probe any further into the question of bowels and their movements.

I still had the sigmoidoscopy left. The instructions that came with the sigmoidoscopy appointment said it was necessary to have a liquid meal instead of solid food the evening before the examination.

I worried about this for days. What constituted a liquid meal? Was carrot juice or blended soup a liquid? Could I cook and puree fish and leeks and garlic? Was ice cream a liquid? It certainly seems to melt into fluid. Was this the moment to indulge in a chocolate gelato?

I rang the clinic to clear up the question. The answer was depressing. Clear broth.

'I think you should word the instructions more clearly,' I said to the woman on the telephone. 'Other people must have rung with this query.'

'You're the first,' she said, firmly.

Father

I had a bad experience this week. I called my eighty-four-year-old father, in Australia. It was 8.30 a.m. for him.

As soon as he answered the phone, I knew I'd woken him up. His voice was groggy. His Polish-Jewish accent was thicker. More pronounced. Still, he sounded pleased to hear from me.

'I woke you up,' I said.

'No, no,' he protested. 'I am still in bed, but I wasn't asleep.'

'You don't sound awake,' I said.

'I am,' he said, sounding as though he was slipping back into sleep.

I felt worried. Something was not right with him. 'Your voice sounds funny, Dad,' I said.

'I can change phones,' he said.

One of his phones has been playing up for weeks. 'No, I'll call you back in five minutes,' I said. 'It will give you time to wake up properly.'

'My dad sounds strange,' I said to my husband.

'He always sounds strange in the mornings,' my husband said. 'Like a subdued Henry Kissinger.'

'He's not himself,' I said. 'And he's not Henry Kissinger. Something has happened.'

I started to panic. I hit redial on the phone and called my father back. He sounded better. More alert. 'Hello, hello, it's nice to hear you,' he said. Then he lapsed. His voice sounded wistful, and a bit breathless.

I felt sick. 'What did you do today?' my father said to me, in a voice that had almost slipped away. I felt as though he was disappearing. I ran out to find my husband.

'Something is wrong with my dad,' I whispered, with urgency, to my husband.

'David wants to speak to you,' I said to my father. 'Okay,' said my father.

'I love you, Dad,' I said.

'I love you, too,' he replied.

I gave the phone to my husband. My heart was pounding. I felt bilious. My husband talked to my father for several minutes. He gave him news of our two daughters, and talked about a current political issue. I paced the apartment.

I was starting to calm down when I heard my husband say, 'What's your name?' slowly to my father. A minute later, my husband said 'What's my name?' in the same slow tones.

I started to tremble. I knew something terrible had happened to my father. I tried, frantically, to think of what I could do. I felt so far away.

Half a minute later, my husband hung up the phone. He walked over to me. 'That wasn't your father,' he said. 'You dialled the wrong number.'

I didn't believe him. 'Of course it was my father,' I said. 'I spoke to him for ten minutes.'

'It was someone else,' my husband said. 'He wouldn't give me his name.'

I hit redial again. The number that came up on the phone was not my father's number. I had misdialled the last digit. My father lives in a Jewish area. Most of his neighbours are Jewish. I must have got someone else's Polish-Jewish father.

I still couldn't quite believe it. I dialled my father's number. My father answered. He sounded like himself. Buoyant. Energetic. Effervescent. I was so happy to hear his voice, I burst into tears.

I told him the whole story. Halfway through, he started to laugh. He couldn't stop laughing. He had to leave the phone to get a tissue. His eyes were streaming.

'Who could I have been speaking to?' I said to my father, when he eventually stopped laughing.

'You've got his number,' he said. 'Should I ring him?'

'No,' I said. 'He sounded quite boring.'

'Did he ask you who you were?' my father asked.

'No,' I said. 'He seemed pleased to hear from me, though. He said he loved me.'

My father started laughing again. He laughed so hard he couldn't speak. I started to laugh, too.

'I'm so glad you're my father,' I said to him. 'I like you much better than I like him.'

Snacking

Americans, it seems, are constantly eating. You can see this in the streets or in movie theatres. They also eat and drink in church, in the classroom, in the office and in the car.

Americans now see eating as something to be done while they are doing something else, a marketing professor from Northwestern University was quoted as saying in an article in the *New York Times*.

Most American cars have cup holders in the front and back. Some cars have refrigerated glove boxes. The Samsung corporation, the *New York Times* said, is marketing the first microwave for cars and minivans. The microwave will plug into the cigarette lighter.

It's easy to snack in America. You can buy and eat food just about anywhere. In libraries, theatres, furniture stores, bookstores. Retail outlets have realised what a boon to business selling coffee and snacks can be.

I can understand a need for a snack. I know what it

feels like to feel insecure without a snack. I shipped some dried carrots to myself before the beginning of my first book tour of Austria and Germany a couple of years ago. I was nervous about the tour. I didn't want to find myself devouring poppy-seed cake or apple strudel out of tension and anxiety.

The dried carrots, I thought, would be perfect. There's a limit to the damage you can do with a dried carrot overdose. I shipped myself four packets.

A week later, I ran into a snag. A Mr Nowak, an Austrian customs official, had seized my carrots. He had called my publisher in Vienna and demanded to know what the packets, which were clearly labelled, contained.

'Dried carrots,' she said. He didn't believe her.

'Does he think it's cocaine disguised as carrot flakes?' I said to my publisher.

'I don't know,' she answered.

'Does your author think we have no carrots in Austria?' Mr Nowak asked my publisher.

'I can't travel with a huge bag of carrots,' I said to her.

Mr Nowak was adamant. I could not have my dried carrots. He confiscated the vitamins I'd shipped over as well. You can bring vitamins into Austria in person, but you cannot ship them.

I managed the book tour without the carrots and without the vitamins. Mr Nowak, had, in fact, inadvertently done me a favour. He'd weaned me off my dried-carrot addiction.

Maybe I should forge a closer connection with Mr Nowak? He could cure me of the need to pack food every time I take a trip. For the two-and-a-half-hour bus ride to Shelter Island, a place I commute to on weekends in the summer, I make a list of what to pack.

'Water for the bus,' I write on my list. I'm not sure why I have to be so specific. Why don't I just write 'Water'? I don't know. But every week I write 'Water for the bus'. Twice. Going there and coming back.

If I catch the 6.30 p.m. bus from New York, the lists can get very long. I eat my dinner on the 6.30 p.m. bus. I take roasted red peppers, corn, grilled eggplant and fresh bread.

Others also eat on the bus. Some people bring multiple hamburgers and packets of fries, or pizza and bags of doughnuts. They are usually men. I'm almost mesmerised watching them chew their way through a cheeseburger or chocolate-covered doughnut.

I admire the ability to eat this sort of food openly. I think I'd be trying to hide the cheeseburgers and chips and doughnuts. And probably choking in an effort not to be detected.

Maybe it's because I'm female? It's harder, I think, for women to sit down to a large helping of unhealthy food. Or maybe a large helping of any food. Maybe it's because we're still trying to be ladylike?

I am. I sit on the bus with a napkin on my lap and take small mouthfuls. I do this out of fear of spilling my food. And looking greedy. And untidy. It's absurd. Really absurd.

'Eat with more abandon,' I plan to write to myself at the end of my next list.

New Yorkers

It's easy to distinguish a real New Yorker from a recently arrived denizen or a transient resident.

Real New Yorkers are obsessed with the idea of leaving New York. A true New Yorker is one who's consumed by thoughts of how to get out of the city. Fixated by how to get away.

When you overhear a conversation about how dementing the city is, you know the participants live here permanently. Conversations about having to get away are commonplace.

All over the city New Yorkers are plotting and hatching and making plans to escape. At any time of the day or night it's not hard to find a New Yorker expressing a desperation to get away. To get away from the city. To get away from the stress. Away from the tension. To get away from the job, the boss, the crowds, the competition. There is so much to get away from.

In this densely populated city, there are the neighbours

to get away from. And there is the apartment. No apartment in the city is ever quite right. Every apartment has its drawbacks.

A friend of mine can hear every sound coming from his neighbours' bedroom. He can hear their lovemaking, and worse, he can hear their arguments. Other than that his apartment is perfect.

If you live in a large building, the sounds from more than one apartment can infiltrate your space. And your psyche. Especially at night. Some people have to drown out neighbouring sounds by producing their own noise. They buy audio cassettes. They sleep to tapes of ocean waves crashing on to shores or tapes of jungle or forest or mountain sounds.

It's quite bizarre to have to sleep accompanied by the noise of chimpanzees running up and down trees in a rainforest when you're in the middle of Manhattan.

Something almost equally bizarre as sleeping to wildlife sounds, is the music that is forced on you in most New York cafes and restaurants.

In the East Village you have to endure dance tracks with the sort of synthesised drumbeat that would be put to good use as a torture implement. The synthesised music is only marginally worse than hearing Vivaldi's *Four Seasons* in every second eating establishment.

I don't know why the music is necessary. You can't hear yourself speak in many cafes and the noise is deafening in most New York restaurants. The crowds and the background music make conversation at less than screaming pitch impossible.

The city's noise is definitely something that real New Yorkers want to get away from.

I knew I belonged here when I realised I was always

making plans to escape. I've been to places I'd never have gone to if I hadn't had such a need to get out of New York City.

I've been to Canada, a country I was entirely indifferent to until it became an alternative to remaining in New York. It was quite interesting.

I've been to the Mojave Desert in California. I'm not the sort of person who goes to deserts. I'm the sort who stays away from them. Deserts seem too desolate and far too deserted for me. The Mojave Desert was not a place I would have rushed to if I wasn't rushing to get away. My husband wanted to go there. I didn't want to stay in New York.

I spent my time in the Mojave Desert horrified that there was no public phone. No cafeteria. No running water. 'It's not as relaxing as Manhattan,' I said to my husband when he excitedly pointed out an enormous mountain goat that was grazing nearby. 'I feel safer in New York,' I said a few minutes later.

And that is the other distinguishing characteristic that makes up a true New Yorker. They hate being away from New York. No place else is good enough. Nothing can compare to the city they've just rushed to leave.

I'm the same. I start missing New York as soon as I decide to go anywhere. I start missing New York when I activate the burglar alarm and double lock my front door.

ALSO BY LILY BRETT AND AVAILABLE IN PICADOR

Just Like That

This is the story of Esther Zepler, modern woman. Happily married wife of artist Sean, and mother of Zachary, Zelda and Kate, she lives in a New York loft, enjoys long lunches with her pregnant friend Sonia, and writes obituaries for a living. But life is never smooth, especially for the daughter of Auschwitz survivors, and her father Edek, communicating via fax and phone from Australia, is an insistent reminder of who she is and where she comes from.

In Full View

'Intimacy is my speciality,' says Lily Brett in one of the remarkable essays in this collection. To the big questions of love and death, sex, motherhood and daughterhood, work, the pleasures of food (and its shadow, body size), Lily Brett now brings the descriptive clarity and hypodermic precision familiar from her novels and poems.

In all her work, Lily Brett's Magnetic North is the Holocaust. Her parents were both death camp survivors, the shipwrecked remains of large families obliterated by the Nazis. Inevitably, Lily's own life was bent and pockmarked by the unfathomable horror of their experience. How she slowly learned to pick her way through keeps the reader excitedly turning these pages, wanting more.

In Full View is hilarious, shrewd, oddly comforting and wise; reading it is like spending time with a uniquely clever, loving and sympathetic friend – who is also an enormously gifted writer.

Too Many Men

*It means 'too many men', a young man passing by said to
Ruth. She is saying to you, you have too many men in your
life. Ruth laughed. Too many men. She didn't have any
men in her life.*

Ruth Rothwax is in control. She keeps her mind sound with
her successful New York-based letter-writing business; she
keeps her body sound by running and lifting weights.
There's no one she has to report to since her three
marriages ended. A good life, all in all . . . But there's
something missing.

Ruth has a burning need to travel with her father Edek to
Poland. She needs him to help her make sense of the
past – to make sense of the murder of her family. She
needs him to help her understand who she is.

So why are people staring at her as if they've seen a
ghost?

Too Many Men is Lily Brett's most powerful and imaginative
novel to date, a dazzling exploration of the places between
past and present, tragedy and comedy, sanity and lunacy. It
is the novel that confirms Lily Brett's status as one of
Australia's wittiest and most loved writers.